GEORGIA
ADVENTURES

GEORGIA ADVENTURES

One-Day and Weekend Getaways

JEFF KUNERTH
AND
DON MELVIN

RUTLEDGE HILL PRESS
Nashville, Tennessee

*This book
is dedicated with love
to Jaime and Jennifer
and
Chad and Jesse.
May your travels be long
and filled with wonder.*

Copyright © 1994 by Jeff Kunerth and Don Melvin

Published in Nashville, Tennessee, by Rutledge Hill Press,
211 Seventh Avenue North, Nashville, Tennessee 37219.

Typesetting by D&T/Bailey Typography, Inc., Nashville, Tennessee

Photograph Credits: pp. 2, 4, 17, 26, 102, 136, 138, 163, 173, 177 courtesy of the Georgia Department of Industry, Trade, and Tourism; p. 8 courtesy of the Atlanta History Center; p. 30 courtesy of Callaway Gardens; p. 54 courtesy of the Macon-Bibb County Convention and Visitors Bureau; p. 113 courtesy of Chateau Elan Winery; p. 116 courtesy of the Augusta-Richmond County Convention and Visitors Bureau; p. 140 courtesy of the Greater Rome Convention and Visitors Bureau; p. 143 courtesy of Berry College; p.163 courtesy of the Savannah Area Convention and Visitors Bureau; pp. 183, 186, 199, 203, 206 courtesy of the Chattanooga News Bureau. All other photographs are by the authors.

Library of Congress Cataloging-in-Publication Data

Kunerth, Jeff.
    Georgia adventures : one-day and weekend getaways / Jeff Kunerth and Don Melvin.
        p.   cm.
    Includes index.
    ISBN 1-55853-321-4
    1. Georgia—Guidebooks.   I. Melvin, Don, 1953–   . II. Title.
F284.3.K86   1994
917.5804'43—dc20   94-32170
                                                                         CIP

Printed in the United States of America
1 2 3 4 5 6 7 8 — 99 98 97 96 95 94

CONTENTS

Georgia

INTRODUCTION

WELCOME TO GEORGIA, BASTION OF THE Confederacy and cradle of the civil rights movement.

That kind of dissonance and diversity, more than any other trait, characterizes the state. Georgia is saturated with history, yet thoroughly modern, a treasury of Civil War sites and the site of the 1996 Olympics. It is home to one of the country's major cities, yet it is covered by thousands of acres of virgin forest. It has mountains and plains and seashore.

Georgia is, after all, the largest state east of the Mississippi. With 58,910 square miles, Georgia is twenty percent larger than New York, thirty percent larger than Pennsylvania, and forty-five percent larger than Virginia.

Georgia reaches from its southeast coast on the Atlantic Ocean up past Atlanta, which lies due south of Detroit. A visitor can hike the Appalachian Mountains, raft down the Chattahoochee River, or bask on the southern beaches.

The state's history stretches from the 1,000-year-old Etowah Indian mounds to the modern skyscrapers of Atlanta. Jimmy Carter was born here and Franklin Roosevelt died here, near Warm Springs where he came to treat the polio that had withered his legs. From the Civil War to civil rights, from the Confederate prison camp at Andersonville to the birthplace of Martin Luther King, Jr., Georgia is dotted with historic sites of national importance.

This is an idiosyncratic book. We have emphasized the places we enjoyed and those we found interesting or moving. We have given most attention to places that make Georgia unique. If we have devoted only a few paragraphs to the enormous Six Flags amusement park while speaking at greater length of Auburn Avenue, it is by design. Amusement parks are everywhere; there is only one Auburn Avenue.

The history of the Civil War has seeped into the land and, indeed, even into the psyche of Georgia. Blood was spilled on this ground. Perhaps the most famous military campaign ever waged on American soil was fought here: Sherman's march from Chattanooga to Atlanta guaranteed Lincoln's re-election. His march from Atlanta to Savannah assured the Union of victory.

But a visit to Georgia does not have to be a trip into the past. You can hang glide off Lookout Mountain or raft the white waters of the Chattooga River, on which _Deliverance_ was filmed.

We have included a chapter on Chattanooga, as it is only two hours from Atlanta and holds much to entertain and amuse visitors.

The book begins with the Atlanta area, and the chapters that follow are organized by region. Mileages are from downtown Atlanta, although the directions may be from the nearest city in the region. Some words of caution: Prices and hours of operation often change without notice. Call ahead to be sure; we have provided the phone numbers. "Handicapped access" means the site, or at least a good part of it, is accessible to wheelchairs. The restrooms may or may not be accessible.

We'd like you to think of this guide as a starting point. Use it to discover the subtleties and richness of Georgia. You may pick, for example, a destination in the northeast mountains; then, if you're overcome by the spirit of adventure, turn down a side road and see what you find. Diamonds in the rough seem to shine more brightly when you unearth them unexpectedly.

CHAPTER ONE

ATLANTA

MANY WHO HAVE NEVER VISITED ATLANTA
know it only from *Gone With the Wind*. Indeed, the novel affected
even Atlanta's view of itself. But we wager that today you'll see
precious few hoop skirts and even fewer blockade runners sporting
pencil-thin mustaches.

Instead, you will find a modern city of gleaming skyscrapers.
Many were designed by Atlanta architect John Portman, whose
fondness for the external elevator will quickly become apparent.

Modern Atlanta is dominated by two men: Ted Turner and
Jimmy Carter. Each has built a monument to himself. Turner,
sometimes called the Mouth of the South, has found in Cable News
Network (CNN) a way to make his voice heard around the world.
The CNN Center Tour draws about 200,000 visitors each year.
Carter's shrine is, characteristically, more understated. But a visit to
the Jimmy Carter Library and Museum, a worthwhile trip, shows
that he too holds himself in high esteem.

Another of Atlanta's claims to fame is its role in the civil rights
movement. Martin Luther King, Jr., was born here, preached here,
and is entombed here. A visit to Auburn Avenue, a center of black
achievement for the better part of this century, will give you a feel
for where the youngest Nobel Peace Prize winner was raised.

Beyond that, you can shop at Underground Atlanta, or frolic
at the Six Flags Over Georgia amusement park. Atlanta's museums
of science, art, and history will entertain and inform you.

And if you truly want to know what Atlanta was like in the
nineteenth century, beyond the hoop skirts and the pencil-thin
mustaches, the Atlanta History Center offers a historical feat for
the senses and the mind.

1

The old South and the new: Atlanta blends the floral beauty long associated with the South with gleaming new high-rises.

Auburn Avenue/Martin Luther King, Jr., Center for Nonviolent Social Change and King Birthplace

Downtown

From north of Atlanta: Take Interstate 75/85 south into the city. Get off at the Butler Street exit. Go straight to the second light. Turn left onto Auburn Avenue. The Martin Luther King, Jr., Center for Nonviolent Social Change is 1 mile ahead on the right.

From south of Atlanta: Take Interstate 75/85 north into the city. Get off at the Edgewood Avenue exit. Go straight to the second light. Turn right onto Auburn Avenue. The King Center is on your right.

From either east or west of Atlanta: Take Interstate 20 into the city. Get off at the Boulevard exit. Turn north on Boulevard (a left turn if you are coming from the west; a right if you are coming from the east). Stay on Boulevard until it intersects Auburn Avenue. The King Center is on your left.

AUBURN AVENUE HAS BECOME A PLACE OF pilgrimage for many African Americans. The house in which Martin Luther King, Jr., was born stands a block from the crypt in which his body lies, and only a block and a half from Ebenezer Baptist Church, where he preached. More than three million people visit each year.

The King home and tomb are the big draws, but there is far more here than that. The district was a center of black entrepreneurial activity in the days before integration. In the 1930s, it was dubbed "Sweet Auburn" because money flowed through here like

Martin Luther King, Jr., was born in this wood frame house on Atlanta's famed Auburn Avenue. The home is within walking distance of his tomb and Ebenezer Baptist Church, where he preached.

honey. In 1957, *Fortune* magazine called Auburn Avenue "the richest Negro street in the world"; the area still evokes the sights and sounds of a vibrant slice of black history.

To tour the district is to understand that, although King was an exceptional man, he was also a product of Sweet Auburn: He rose from a tradition of accomplishment.

We recommend a walking tour, starting where Auburn Avenue crosses Courtland Street. Head east, away from downtown, with the skyscrapers at your back. On each side of the street, notice the brown "Freedom Walk" historical markers that identify buildings of historical importance.

And there are plenty. The Atlanta Life Insurance Company, founded in 1905 by a former slave, is still thriving today. The *Atlanta Daily World*, the oldest black-owned daily newspaper in the country, continues to publish. WERD, the first black-owned radio station, is now defunct. The Prince Hall Masonic building, which since 1965 has housed the national headquarters of the Southern

Christian Leadership Conference, can be found here, among many other notable buildings.

Stop in the APEX (African American Panoramic Experience) museum. Visitors can watch a seventeen-minute videotape on the history of Auburn Avenue. The museum displays African art and rotating exhibits of local and national black artists. A welcome center in the museum offers information about Atlanta's black-oriented restaurants, nightclubs, art stores, and tourist attractions.

Visitors are welcome in Ebenezer Baptist Church, where King preached, as did his father and grandfather before him. On weekdays, you can sit in the pews and hear a tape recording detailing the history of the church. Attending regular Sunday services, which feature rollicking gospel music and powerful preaching, is a moving and joyful experience.

King's marble tomb lies above cascading waters at the Martin Luther King, Jr., Center for Nonviolent Social Change. Mementos of King's life, such as his Nobel Peace Prize, are here. Videotapes show histories of the civil rights movement. A gift shop sells books on King and other black leaders.

The King Center is also where you sign up for National Park Service tours of the King birthplace. The King home is interesting, partly as a period piece, partly because the guides tell amusing tales of King's youthful naughtiness.

MARTIN LUTHER KING, JR., CENTER FOR NONVIOLENT
SOCIAL CHANGE
449 Auburn Avenue
Atlanta, GA 30312
(404) 524-1956; For information about tours of the King
home, call (404) 526-8944.

HOURS: 9 A.M. to 7 P.M., seven days a week between Labor Day
and Memorial Day. Winter hours are 9 A.M. to 5:30 P.M.
ADMISSION: Free.
HANDICAPPED ACCESS: Yes. FOOD: Yes.
RESTROOMS: Yes.

EBENEZER BAPTIST CHURCH
407 Auburn Avenue, NE
Atlanta, GA 30312
(404) 688-7263

HOURS: Sunday services at 7:45 A.M. and 10:45 A.M. On other days, visitors are welcome between 9:30 A.M. and 4:30 P.M.
ADMISSION: Free (donations accepted).
HANDICAPPED ACCESS: No.
FOOD: No.
RESTROOMS: No.

APEX MUSEUM
135 Auburn Avenue, NE
Atlanta, GA 30303
(404) 521-APEX

HOURS: Tuesday through Saturday, 10 A.M. to 5 P.M. In June, July, August, and February, APEX is open on Sunday, from 1 P.M. to 5 P.M. Closed Monday.
ADMISSION: Adults, $2; Students, $1; Seniors 55 and older, $1; Children 1–4, free.
FOOD: No.
RESTROOMS: Yes.

Atlanta History Center
Northeast Atlanta

From downtown Atlanta: Take Interstate 75 north. Get off at Exit 107 (West Paces Ferry Road). At the end of the ramp, turn left onto Northside Parkway, then right at the light onto West Paces Ferry Road. After 2.5 miles, turn right onto Andrews Drive. (Ignore all other roads named Andrews.) Take the first driveway on the left to the history center.

THE ATLANTA HISTORY CENTER IS WELL WORTH the two hours or so it takes to visit. You cannot feel and touch and see and smell the history of Atlanta fully at any other single location. Located on thirty-two acres of prime real estate, the center shows life in the Atlanta area before, during, and after the Civil War—and on into the present.

The main museum, an 83,000-square-foot museum where your visit begins, houses a superb Civil War exhibit of more than six hundred artifacts. Here you can see a wooden wagon used by Sherman in the Atlanta campaign. Swords, guns, uniforms, ammunition, and flags adorn the walls and fill the cases. If you have time, take the guided tour of the Civil War exhibit. The guides do not regurgitate a canned spiel; instead, they provide a fine overview of the war, salted with excellent interpretation. (One result of the South's impromptu bring-your-own-weapon army: difficulty in supplying everyone with ammunition of the proper caliber. One motivation for Sherman's determination to capture Atlanta: he was tired of seeing MADE IN ATLANTA stamped on Confederate munitions he captured.)

The museum also houses an exhibit on Atlanta's resurgence. The city devastated by the war transformed itself into a scene of the civil rights movement, and into the modern city able to host the 1994 Super Bowl and the 1996 Summer Olympic Games.

The Swan House at the Atlanta History Center—so named for the swan motif in its decor—affords a glimpse of the life lived by Atlanta's wealthy earlier this century.

Elsewhere on the grounds is the Tullie Smith House. Built in 1833, it is one of the few pre-Civil War Atlanta houses still standing. It was part of a prosperous, if not wealthy, plantation: the occupants owned 800 acres and 11 slaves. Yet even for the prosperous, life in the early 1800s was spartan. Sheep and chickens live in the outbuildings. Inside the house, you can see wool spun into yarn. Other outbuildings house demonstrations of cooking and storing of food at the turn of the century.

For life after the war, take a guided tour of the Swan House, so named for all the swans carved, painted, etched, and otherwise emblazoned throughout. Built in 1928, the mansion is ornate and luxurious. The floor of the foyer is black and white marble. A dramatic spiral staircase dominates the house. Some of the furniture is European, dating from the early 1700s.

Trails meander throughout the woods and gardens of the center; markers identify certain plants and trees. The Swan Coach House, the former servants' quarters, houses a restaurant and gift shop.

ATLANTA HISTORY CENTER
3101 Andrews Drive, NW
Atlanta, GA 30305
(404) 814-4000

HOURS: Monday through Saturday, 9 A.M. to 5:30 P.M.; Sunday, noon to 5:30 P.M. The center is closed, or the hours limited, on major holidays.

ADMISSION: Adults, $6.50; Seniors 65 and older, $5; Students, $5; Children 6–17, $4; Children 5 and younger, free.

HANDICAPPED ACCESS: Mostly, although the second floor of the Swan House is not.

FOOD: Swan Coach House Restaurant is open from 11:30 A.M. until 2:30 P.M.

RESTROOMS: Yes.

CNN Studio Tour

Downtown

Located in the Omni complex at the corner of Techwood Drive and Marietta Street. Parking is available at the Cable News Network (CNN) Center parking decks across from the complex, or take MARTA, the subway system, to the Omni stop.

From north of Atlanta: Take Interstate 75/85 south into the city. Get off at Exit 99 (Williams Street). Follow the blue signs to the World Congress Center. The CNN Center is in the same complex.

From south of Atlanta: Take Interstate 75/85 north into the city. Get off at Exit 96 (International Boulevard). Follow the blue signs to the World Congress Center. The CNN Center is in the same complex.

IF THE JIMMY CARTER LIBRARY AND MUSEUM IS Carter's quiet and subdued monument to himself, then Cable News Network, the voice heard around the world, is Ted Turner's monument to *himself*. Come and tour the network that Ted built. Mostly this involves looking down through glass at a live broadcast as a guide describes how the news is gathered and who sits where. Check out the anchor desk. You'll see debris—notes, books, a hair brush, perhaps a hand-held mirror—that you never see on the air.

You'll discover that TV weather forecasters do not stand in front of a map. Instead, they wave their arms in front of a blank blue wall. Blue tells the computer to insert the graphics; off-screen monitors let the personalities know where to point. You can try it yourself. But if you're wearing a blue shirt, you'll look at the monitor and find a weather map where your torso ought to be, which explains why you never see weather forecasters wearing blue shirts.

This is a popular tour, so it's best to arrive early. The tour lasts about fifty minutes, and you'll descend several flights of stairs. You must buy a ticket for a certain time. If you come later in the day, you may find yourself with a couple of hours or more to wait. If so, Underground Atlanta is not far. Or, the CNN Center houses a number of shops and fast-food joints. Also here is the Turner Store. You can buy books about CNN, CNN hats, CNN ties. Turner owns 6,700 films; you can buy *Gone With the Wind* mugs, clocks, pillows, etc., or souvenirs of other movies, such as *The Wizard of Oz*.

CNN STUDIO TOUR
One CNN Center
P.O. Box 105366
Atlanta, GA 30348-5366
(404) 827-2300

HOURS: Tours are conducted every half-hour between 9 A.M. and 5 P.M., seven days a week. Tickets go on sale at 8:30 A.M. and can only be used on the day of purchase. Closed Thanksgiving, Christmas Eve and Christmas Day, New Year's, Easter, Memorial Day, July 4, and Labor Day.
ADMISSION: Adults, $6; Seniors 65 and older, $4; Children 6–12, $3.50; Children 5 and younger, free.
HANDICAPPED ACCESS: 24-hour advance notice required.
FOOD: Fast-food restaurants.
RESTROOMS: Yes.

Fernbank Museum of Natural History

East Atlanta

From downtown: Go north on Peachtree Street. Turn right onto Ponce De Leon Avenue, at the Fox Theater. Continue past Boulevard, Highland Avenue, and Moreland Avenue to Clifton Road. Turn left at the light onto Clifton Road. The museum will be your first right.

 From north of Atlanta: Head toward the city, traveling south on Interstate 75/85. Get off at Exit 100. Turn left onto North Avenue. Turn left onto Piedmont Road. Take your first right onto Ponce De Leon Avenue. Take Ponce De Leon to Clifton Road. Turn left onto Clifton Road. The museum will be your first right.

 From south of Atlanta: Take Interstate 75/85 north into the city. Get off at Exit 91. Take Interstate 20 east to Exit 28 (Moreland Avenue). Turn left onto Moreland Avenue. Continue past Memorial Drive, Inman Park, Dekalb Avenue, and Euclid Avenue to Ponce De Leon Avenue. Turn right onto Ponce De Leon, and follow it for four lights to Clifton Road. Turn left onto Clifton. The museum will be your first right.

IF NATURE INSPIRES AWE IN YOU, OR EVEN MILD curiosity, a visit to the Fernbank Museum of Natural History is time well spent. "A Walk Through Time in Georgia," the major exhibit, begins with a short film illustrating the creation of Earth according to the Big Bang Theory. The exhibits that follow are realistic enough to excite young and old. They range from dinosaurs to animals that inhabit various regions of modern Georgia.

 The Okeefenokee Swamp, for example, is reproduced complete with a submerged alligator, a snake, a bobcat, and birds. Every four minutes the swamp goes through one twenty-four-hour cycle. The light fades, the birds twitter, swamp things croak—and children and adults are transfixed. Other regions of the state are replicated as well.

Another fine exhibit is the "Spectrum of the Senses," a hall filled with dozens of do-it-yourself illusions designed to illustrate scientific principles. Warning: It will take a long time to drag your children out.

It costs extra, but don't miss the IMAX movie theater. The screen—seventy feet high and fifty-two feet across—makes you feel part of the scene, even to the point of inducing motion sickness in a few people. But fear not: If you feel ill, close your eyes. The sensation of motion stops at once.

FERNBANK MUSEUM OF NATURAL HISTORY
767 Clifton Road, NE
Atlanta, GA 30307-1221
(404) 378-0127

HOURS: Monday through Saturday, 9 A.M. to 6 P.M.; Sunday, noon to 6 P.M.
ADMISSION: Museum: Adults, $5.50; Seniors 55 and older, $4.50; Children 3 through college age (with student ID), $4.50.
IMAX THEATER: Same prices as for the museum. However, you can buy a single ticket that will admit you to both for $9.50, adults, and $7.50 for seniors, children, and students.
HANDICAPPED ACCESS: Yes.
FOOD: Yes.
RESTROOMS: Yes. (Men's and women's restrooms in the entry lobby have diaper-changing tables.)

Fernbank Science Center
East Atlanta

Follow the directions to the Fernbank Museum of Natural History until you are on Ponce De Leon Avenue. Continue straight, past Clifton Road. Turn left onto Artwood Road, then right onto Heaton Park Drive.

HIDDEN HERE FOR THOSE WHO KNOW HOW TO look are screech owls, mourning doves, wood thrushes, raccoons, rabbits, and even the occasional copperhead. The forest is encircled now by the city it once surrounded. It has become an oasis—quiet nourishment for the soul amid the noise of the city.

The 65 acres of Fernbank Forest make up the largest undisturbed piece of piedmont (foot-of-mountain) forest in a city. Wild ginger still blooms purple on the ground. Two miles of paved trails lead through the woods. An easy-effort trail has been created for those with physical impairments, with a guide rope for the vision impaired.

The exhibition hall houses several displays. Among them: a dinosaur exhibit showing life in prehistoric Atlanta; a model of the Okeefenokee Swamp; the real Apollo 6 capsule; and the birds of Fernbank Forest. In addition, there is a 500-seat planetarium.

FERNBANK SCIENCE CENTER
156 Heaton Park Drive
Atlanta, GA 30307
(404) 378-4311

HOURS: Monday, 8:30 A.M. to 5 P.M.; Tuesday through Friday, 8:30 A.M. to 10 P.M.; Saturday, 10:30 A.M. to 5 P.M.; Sunday 1 P.M. to 5 P.M.

ADMISSION: Exhibition hall and forest, free. For adults' shows, the planetarium fees are: Adults, $2; Children 6 and older, $1; Students, $1; Seniors 62 and older, free. Admittance to children's shows costs fifty cents per person.

HANDICAPPED ACCESS: Yes.

FOOD: No.

RESTROOMS: Yes.

Georgia Governor's Mansion

Northeast Atlanta

From downtown Atlanta: Take Interstate 75 north. Take Exit 107 (West Paces Ferry Road). Turn left onto Northside Parkway, then right onto West Paces Ferry Road. The mansion will be on your left after about 1 mile.

THE GOVERNOR'S MANSION IS LOCATED IN Buckhead, one of Atlanta's most beautiful neighborhoods, where the lots go for $1 million an acre—sans house. Enjoy the drive. Then you can proceed to the Atlanta History Center, just down the road, and tour Atlanta's past.

White columns surround the mansion, in the Greek Revival style so closely associated with antebellum southern mansions. Was the home built by a wealthy slaveholder? The lord of a large plantation? No. It opened in the 1960s, and it was first occupied by Lester Maddox, the restaurateur who passed out ax handles to his white clientele so they could fend off black would-be customers, and who parlayed that bit of infamy into the governorship.

Although the mansion dates back less than thirty years, historic furnishings abound inside. You can see the family living room, the family dining room, the state dining room, and the library. Most are graced with beautiful nineteenth-century furniture, and the house itself is lovely, no matter who built it.

Beware: You will be kicked out precisely at closing time. Perhaps the governor's family gets tired of sitting outside in the car.

GEORGIA GOVERNOR'S MANSION
391 West Paces Ferry Road, NE
Atlanta, GA 30305
(404) 261-1776

HOURS: Tuesday, Wednesday, and Thursday, 10 A.M. to 11:30 A.M.
ADMISSION: Free.
HANDICAPPED ACCESS: Yes.
FOOD: No.
RESTROOMS: No.

Jimmy Carter
Library and Museum

East Atlanta

*Take Interstate 75/85 into the city. Get off at Exit 96
(Carter Center). Follow the signs to the Carter Center.*

THE MUSEUM IS TASTEFULLY DONE. FROM THE
outside it appears modest, reflecting Jimmy Carter's personality.
Still, this is Carter's monument to himself, and the modesty is
limited to the exterior. Banners hanging from the ceiling proclaim
him "National Leader," "Conservationist," "Reformer," "Peace-
maker," "World Leader," "Problem Solver," and "Commander in
Chief."

A replica of the Oval Office, furnished as it was during Carter's
presidency, is one of the more interesting exhibits. Carter's disem-
bodied voice narrates: After his inauguration he had trouble realiz-
ing the office was his, and that he could touch things, move things,
draw the drapes. And he speaks of his final days as president: He
never left the Oval Office as he worked around the clock to
negotiate the freedom of U.S. hostages held in Iran, grabbing a few
minutes of sleep on the sofa.

Another exhibit allows visitors to respond to a terrorist threat.
Should you attack? Negotiate? Apply sanctions? Press the button,
and Carter will tell you how your choice would have affected the
United States.

On display are gifts the Carters received from the shah of Iran,
Israeli prime minister Menachem Begin, and others.

JIMMY CARTER LIBRARY AND MUSEUM
One Copenhill
Atlanta, GA 30307
(404) 331-0296 or (404) 331-3942

The Jimmy Carter Library and Museum houses memorabilia and exhibits from the presidency of Georgia's most famous peanut farmer.

HOURS: Monday through Saturday, 9 A.M. to 4:45 P.M.; Sunday, noon to 4:45 P.M. Closed Thanksgiving, Christmas, and New Year's.

ADMISSION: Adults, $2.50; Seniors 55 and older, $1.50; Children 15 and younger, free.

HANDICAPPED ACCESS: Yes. Wheelchairs available.

FOOD: A cafe is open from 11 A.M. to 4 P.M.

RESTROOMS: Yes.

SciTrek

Downtown

From north of Atlanta: Take Interstate 75/85 south into the city. Get off at Exit 97 (Courtland Avenue/Georgia State University). At the second light, turn left onto Harris Street. At the first light, turn left onto Piedmont Avenue. SciTrek will be two and one-half blocks down on your right.

From south of Atlanta: Take Interstate 75/85 north into the city. Get off at Exit 95A (Piedmont/Baker Street), which peels off from the lefthand lane of the interstate. Go straight on Piedmont, across Baker. SciTrek will be one and one-half blocks down on your right.

SCITREK, THE SCIENCE AND TECHNOLOGY MUseum of Atlanta, boasts more than 100 interactive exhibits, each designed to illustrate a scientific principle. Magnetic repulsion? Switch the magnet on and watch it fire an aluminum disc fifteen feet into the air. Similar displays illustrate electricity, levers, gyroscopes, and the like. Periodically, more elaborate demonstrations are staged; they are announced over the loud speaker in time for visitors to gather.

SciTrek was ranked in 1991 by *Good Housekeeping* magazine as one of the top 10 science centers in the nation. Children love it for its many hands-on exhibits. A special area entertains younger children. Touring exhibits come from other parts of the country and may cover anything from sharks to holography.

However, many of the regular exhibits are similar to those in the Fernbank Museum of Natural History's "Spectrum of the Senses." And Fernbank has additional attractions: "A Walk Through Time in Georgia," featuring huge dinosaurs, and (though it costs extra) the huge, stomach-churning IMAX movie screen. If you have to choose one, we recommend Fernbank.

SCITREK
395 Piedmont Avenue
Atlanta, GA 30308
(404) 522-5500

HOURS: Tuesday through Saturday, 10 A.M. to 5 P.M.; Sunday, noon through 5 P.M. Closed Easter, Thanksgiving, Christmas, and New Year's.

ADMISSION: Adults, $6.50; Children 3–17, $4.25; College students with ID, $4.25; Seniors 65 and older, $4.25. After 2 P.M., from September through May, admission is $3.75. Parking costs $4.

HANDICAPPED ACCESS: Yes.

FOOD: Vending machines sell snacks.

RESTROOMS: Yes.

Shooting the Hooch: Rafting the Chattahoochee River

North Atlanta

To put in at Johnson Ferry, the uppermost point: Take Interstate 75 north out of Atlanta. Go east on Interstate 285. Get off at Exit 16. Turn left at the end of the exit. At the third light, turn left onto Johnson Ferry Road. The embarkation point is on the right, just after you cross over the river.

To put in at Powers Island, the lower point: Take Interstate 75 north out of Atlanta. Go east on Interstate 285. Get off at Exit 15. Turn left at the end of the exit. Go through the first two lights, back over the interstate. Turn left onto the access road. The embarkation point is a half-mile down the road on the right, before you cross the river.

SHOOTING THE HOOCH IS A WONDERFUL WAY to relax away a summer day. Although a good portion of the ride is inside the perimeter (that's Atlantese for inside Interstate 285, which encircles the city), much of the river bank remains forested. Turtles sun themselves on rocks. Ducks paddle upstream. Trout splash through the surface of the water. It is easy to imagine the river as it was one hundred or two hundred years ago, before the interstates were built and the Super Bowl came to town.

More than 130 years ago, some of the Andrews' Raiders dived into this river to escape being hanged for their part in the attempted theft of a Confederate locomotive. The river carried them to the Gulf of Mexico, where they met Union troops (see page 130—Big Shanty Museum).

Two years after that, Gen. William T. Sherman jumped glee-fully—and nudely—into the river. He washed away the dirt he had accumulated since leaving Chattanooga two months earlier, put his clothes back on, and conquered Atlanta.

You can swim here, too, but don't do it nude. Shoes are recommended to protect your feet from the rocky bottom. Sneakers are better than flip-flops, which get stuck in the muck and are an encumbrance when you try to kick your way back aboard your raft. You can rent an inflated rubber raft for four, six, or eight people, or a canoe. Lifejackets and paddles come with the rental, but the river current does most of the work. You're welcome to take a cooler, but rules prohibit Styrofoam and glass.

The water runs faster on some days than on others, but this is a lazy trip. From Johnson Ferry to Powers Island, 6.3 miles, takes about three hours. You can get out there, or continue; from Powers Island to the last take-out point, about 3.8 miles, takes another two hours. Or you can begin in the middle, at Powers Island, and just take the shorter trip.

The upper portion has more riverside real estate. The lower portion is less developed and more scenic, with rocks and shoals that create the vague illusion of rapids.

Reservations are recommended for weekends. A shuttle bus will bring you back to your car when you're done.

CHATTAHOOCHEE OUTDOOR CENTER
1990 Island Ford Parkway
Dunwoody, GA 30350
(404) 395-6851

HOURS: 10 A.M. to 8 P.M. weekdays; 9 A.M. to 8 P.M. weekends and holidays. The Johnson Ferry location will not rent after 1:30 P.M.; the Powers Island location rents until 4:30 P.M. Open seven days a week from Memorial Day to Labor Day, and weekends only for a couple of weeks on either end of that period.

RENTAL: Four-person raft (9 feet), $36; six-person raft (11 feet), $54; eight-person raft (13 feet), $74; canoe, $30. Each rental requires a deposit—$75 per raft, $100 per canoe—unless you have a reservation. The deposit can be covered with cash, personal check, or Visa or MasterCard. Deposits are returned at the point where you rented the raft.

HANDICAPPED ACCESS: Yes.

FOOD: Snacks.

RESTROOMS: Yes, believe it or not. A sign on the riverbank tells you when to pull over to find them.

Six Flags Over Georgia

9 miles

From downtown Atlanta: Go west on Interstate 20. Get off at the Six Flags exit.

THIS IS ONE HUMONGOUS AMUSEMENT PARK. It features rides for kids, rides for adults, and rides for nuts. Ninja, the black belt of roller coasters, for example, will spin you upside down five times.

There are milder rides, too, like Elmer Fudd's Fewis Wheel and Tweety's Swing, both of which are in Loony Tunes Land. There are some water rides, if you don't mind a bit of spray in the face.

The park stages such shows as the Batman Stunt Show; Bugs Bunny's Jumpin', Jammin' Jamboree; and the Wild West Comedy Gunfight Show.

It's a fine park and a big one. For one entrance price you can get your fill of rides and shows; they're all included. Not included, of course, are food, drinks, and merchandise.

SIX FLAGS OVER GEORGIA
P.O. Box 43187
Atlanta, GA 30378
(404) 948-9290

HOURS: Generally, during July and August, the park is open from 10 A.M. to 10 P.M., Sunday through Thursday. Friday and Saturday during that period, often 10 A.M. to midnight. However, hours of operation vary seasonally and change without warning. Call first. Generally not open from November through February.

ADMISSION: Adults: $25 (two-day pass is $28.30); Children 3–9, $18; Children 2 and younger, free; Seniors 55 and older, $14.

HANDICAPPED ACCESS: Yes.

FOOD: Yes.

RESTROOMS: Yes.

Underground Atlanta

Downtown

From south of Atlanta: Go north on Interstate 75/85 into the city. Get off at Exit 91 (Fulton Street/Central Avenue). Follow Central Avenue to Martin Luther King Jr. Drive. Turn left. The parking garages will be on your right.

From north of Atlanta: Go south on Interstate 75/85 into the city. Get off at Exit 93 (Martin Luther King Jr. Drive). Turn right onto Martin Luther King Jr. Drive. The parking garages will be four blocks down on your right.

MANY VISITORS WITH BUT A DAY TO SPEND IN Atlanta make Underground their port of call. It's downtown, it offers more Atlanta clothing and souvenirs than any sane person could want, and something about it seems to say "Atlanta." Perhaps it's the T-shirts and coffee mugs.

Underground is a bunch of boutiques surrounded by a brick-street, turn-of-the-century motif. It is located at Five Points, the site of the railway station that gave this city its earlier, less romantic, name of Terminus. If you read *Gone With the Wind* or saw the movie, this is where the trains disgorge hundreds of wounded Confederate soldiers as Scarlett comes seeking a doctor to deliver Melanie's baby.

This buffet of boutiques is pseudo-history, compared to Auburn Avenue or Andersonville or Kennesaw Mountain. But it is good, air-conditioned family fun, with more than 130 shops and eateries, leavened by the occasional minstrel, juggler, or sword-swallower.

If you have visited Faneuil Hall in Boston, you have the idea.

Just across Central Avenue and the plaza is the World of Coca-Cola. Coke was invented in Atlanta, at a pharmacy a few blocks from here. In 1886, Doc Pemberton stirred some syrup with an oar in his back yard, brought it to his pharmacy, and mixed it with soda water. The potion was meant to cure hangovers. But it grew to become, in the words of journalist William Allen White, "the sublimated essence of all that American stands for." (Coca-Cola world headquarters are in Atlanta still; you can see the building from Interstate 75/85 if you look to the west as you pass the Tenth Street exit.)

The World of Coca-Cola is worth a visit. True, the company has found a way to charge admission to three floors of Coke advertising. But what advertising! It is a chronicle of popular life in America from the turn of the century to the present. Some of the ads may even make you mist up, such as the one in which limping football player Mean Joe Greene tosses his jersey to a small boy who has offered him a Coke, or the one in which singers on a mountaintop in Italy want to buy the world a Coke.

UNDERGROUND ATLANTA
Management Offices
50 Upper Alabama Street
Suite 007
Atlanta, GA 30303
(404) 523-2311

HOURS: Monday through Saturday, 10 A.M. to 9:30 P.M.;
  Sunday, noon to 6 P.M.
ADMISSION: Free.
HANDICAPPED ACCESS: Yes.
FOOD: Plenty of it, and lots of variety.
RESTROOMS: Yes.

THE WORLD OF COCA-COLA
55 Martin Luther King, Jr., Drive
Atlanta, GA 30303
(404) 676-5151

HOURS: Monday through Saturday, 10 A.M. to 9:30 P.M.;
  Sunday, noon to 6 P.M. Admission is cut off one hour before
  closing to ensure that visitors have time to see the entire
  exhibit.
ADMISSION: Adults, $2.50; Seniors 56 and older, $2; Children
  6–12, $1.50; Children 5 and younger, free with adult admis-
  sion.
HANDICAPPED ACCESS: Yes.
FOOD: No.
RESTROOMS: Yes.

Zoo Atlanta/Cyclorama

Downtown

*From the intersection of Interstate 75/85 with Interstate 20
in downtown Atlanta: Take Interstate 20 east one exit. Get
off at Exit 26 (Boulevard). Turn right at the end of the ramp
onto Boulevard. One-half mile on your right is the parking for
Grant Park. Zoo Atlanta and Cyclorama are both in Grant
Park.*

ZOO ATLANTA AND CYCLORAMA ARE WITHIN
spitting distance of each other and can easily be seen in the same
day. If you overheat walking around the zoo, head for the air-
conditioned comfort of the Civil War exhibit. There is a small hot-
dog type restaurant near both entrances, which are practically side
by side. There are picnic areas in Grant Park. (The park, by the
way, was named for Col. Lemuel P. Grant, who built Atlanta's Civil
War fortifications. *Nothing* here is named for Ulysses S. Grant.)

Zoo Atlanta

ZOO ATLANTA IS A MODERN, WELL-MAINTAINED
zoo, free of the cages and odors that characterized zoos of the past.
The animals live outdoors in areas resembling their native habitats.
Feeding times are posted. You can sit inside a small building, look
out through plate glass, and watch a gorilla family eat right in front
of you. Docents dressed in safari gear are stationed throughout the
zoo to answer questions about the animals. Their knowledgeable
answers, along with signs at the exhibits, show the zoo's commit-
ment to preserving endangered species.

The king of beasts gazes nonchalantly at visitors to Zoo Atlanta.

As you enter the zoo, you will be issued a handy little map. You can rent a stroller for $2. Kids can tour the zoo in a small train, which costs $1 per ride. The petting zoo has the usual complement of goats, llamas, and the like.

Don't miss the World of Reptiles. Scores of snakes slither and sleep in nicely re-created habitats. Other reptiles live here as well, and interactive displays are informative. One exhibit purports to show the most ferocious animal in the world, one that consumes 15 million acres of forest each year and kills large numbers of less ferocious species. As you try to peer through the glass to discover what manner of beast this is, you find yourself looking in a mirror. The species, identified as nonvenomous, is Homo sapiens.

ZOO ATLANTA
800 Cherokee Avenue, SE
Atlanta, GA 30315
(404) 624-5600

HOURS: Monday through Friday, 10 A.M. to 4:30 P.M., and the grounds close at 5:30 P.M.; Saturday and Sunday, 10 A.M. to 5:30 P.M., and the grounds close at 6:30 P.M.

ADMISSION: Adults, $7.75; Children 3–11, $5.75; Children 2 and younger, free.

HANDICAPPED ACCESS: Yes.

FOOD: Yes.

RESTROOMS: Yes.

Cyclorama

CYCLORAMA'S MAIN FEATURE IS AN ENORmous one-hundred-year-old, circular painting that depicts the Battle of Atlanta. The painting, 42 feet high and 358 feet in circumference, is the largest in the world. A diorama with soldiers, wagons, railway tracks, and such stands in front of the painting. From your seat it is hard to tell where the diorama ends and the painting begins.

You begin with a short film on the Atlanta campaign boomingly narrated by James Earl Jones. The short version is this: In 1864, Gen. William T. Sherman left Chattanooga, 113 miles north, determined to capture Atlanta, a key southern industrial site and rail center. In pitched battles, the Confederates held the Federals at bay. But again and again, Sherman outflanked the Confederates, threatening to cut the rail line between them and Atlanta. Again and again, the Confederates fell back. Sherman's capture of Atlanta assured Abraham Lincoln of re-election over a candidate who likely would have accepted division of the Union. After the film, you sit on a slowly rotating platform. A narrator describes key parts of the battle of Atlanta as a spotlight shines on the relevant parts of the huge painting. The experience is quite vivid.

Also housed in the building is the Texas, the locomotive that chased another locomotive, the General, in the bizarre Civil War episode that inspired the Disney movie *The Great Locomotive Chase.* (The General is housed in the Big Shanty Museum in Kennesaw. See page 130.)

CYCLORAMA
800 Cherokee Avenue, SE
Atlanta, GA 30315
(404) 624-1071 or (404) 658-7625

HOURS: June 1 through Sept. 30, daily from 9:30 A.M. to 5:30 P.M.; Winter hours are 9:30 A.M. to 4:30 P.M. Closed Christmas, New Year's, Martin Luther King, Jr., Day, and Thanksgiving.

ADMISSION: Adults, $3.50; Seniors 60 and older, $3; Children 6–12, $2; Children 5 and younger, free.

HANDICAPPED ACCESS: Yes.

FOOD: No.

RESTROOMS: Yes.

CHAPTER TWO

THE PLAINS

NATIVE GEORGIANS REFER TO ANYTHING
south of Macon as the "gnat belt." It's where the land flattens out,
the days get hotter, the air seems more moist and languid, and the
bug count goes up. It's the land of pecans, peaches, peanuts, plantations, and presidents.

Still largely rural, the plains of middle and southern Georgia
are where Atlanta's influence peters out. In a state where about
one-third of the counties are considered part of metropolitan Atlanta, the plains are beyond the reach of suburban sprawl.

The plains are the land of small towns, little cities, and large
plantations. It's where the way of life is distinctly slower paced—the
part of Georgia where one president came to relax, and another
president returned to retire.

Making the most of their agricultural heritage, the plains
enshrine the small towns and farms of the past at Westville and
Georgia's Agrirama, as well as several plantations that have been
preserved as museums. The region also has taken some of the land
ravished by time and poor farming practices and converted it into
state parks and vacation retreats in the form of Providence Canyon
and Callaway Gardens.

Although not as majestic as North Georgia, South Georgia is
anything but monotonous. Rural Georgia doesn't overwhelm; instead it surprises you. Like sticking a ridge in the middle of the
flatlands and calling it Pine Mountain, or painting the landscape
with brilliant colors and exotic images and naming it Pasaquan.

Fiercely patriotic, the people of the plains are proud of their
military heritage on land (the National Infantry Museum), in the

air (Museum of Aviation), and on the sea (Confederate Naval Museum). With the same reverence, they honor the casualties of war at the Andersonville National Cemetery.

Georgia poet Sidney Lanier has a big lake named after him north of Atlanta, even though he was born in Macon and received fame writing about the beauty of South Georgia.

Families find plenty to do at Callaway Gardens, including riding their bikes along the 7.5-mile Discovery Bike Path that weaves past the park's multi-colored azalea bushes.

Callaway Gardens

Pine Mountain
86 miles

From Atlanta: Take Interstate 85 south to Exit 5; take Interstate 185 south to Exit 14; take Highway 27 south 10 miles.

SOME COME FOR THE AZALEAS. SOME COME TO see the butterflies. Some come to ogle the Christmas tree lights. And some come to pedal bikes around the lakes and through the woods, whack a golf ball around 63 holes, ride horses, play tennis, swim, fish, or picnic. There's even a permanent circus tent, where, in the summer months, Florida State University's Flying High Circus performs.

It's easy to spend a day at Callaway Gardens. In fact, some people stay the whole week, shelling out $1,650 or more for the resort's popular family vacation packages. While the parents are playing tennis, shooting skeet, or golfing, the kids are swimming, playing ping-pong, riding horses, or canoeing.

For a day trip, the best way to see everything in the 14,300-acre resort is on a bicycle. If you can't bring yours, you can rent one at the Bike Barn. Rentals range from $8 for two hours to $15 a day. A 7.5-mile bike path loops around the lakes to the Day Butterfly Center, where multitudes of butterflies flitter around inside a steamy, glass-enclosed dome; the Azalea trails, where some of the gardens' 700 varieties of azaleas are clustered; and the beach-and-picnic areas on Robin Lake. There are also a huge horticultural center, an elaborate vegetable garden, a log cabin museum, and miles of hiking trails. Paddle boats, sailboats, and canoes are also available for rent.

Started by textile magnate Cason J. Callaway as a form of therapy following a heart attack, the gardens have evolved from one man's private preserve of beauty into a 2,500-acre full-service resort that opened to the public in 1962 after Callaway's death.

The resort's festivities change with the seasons, and so do the admission prices. The spring azalea season, when the gardens are ablaze with blooms, is the most expensive time of the year—$10 per adult, $3 per child. In December, Callaway Gardens' elaborate Christmas light display draws visitors in traffic-jam crowds to see its roads transformed by light and sound.

There are plenty of restaurants in Callaway Gardens, but it's a good idea to make reservations when you arrive.

Perhaps the most impressive thing about Callaway Gardens is that before it was turned into a recreational haven, the land where Cason Callaway planted his first garden was somebody else's played-out cotton field. One man's dust bowl is another man's Eden.

CALLAWAY GARDENS
P.O. Box 2000
Pine Mountain, GA 31822
(706) 663-2281

HOURS: January and February, 8 A.M. to 5 P.M.; March, 7 A.M. to 6 P.M.; April to September, 7 A.M. to 7 P.M.; October, 8 A.M. to 6 P.M.; November, 8 A.M. to 5 P.M.; December, 8 A.M. to 4 P.M.

ADMISSION: October to February: Adults, $7.50; Children, $1.50; March: Adults, $10; Children, $3; April to September: Adults, $8.50; Children, $2.50.

HANDICAPPED ACCESS: Yes.

FOOD: Snack bars and restaurants.

RESTROOMS: Yes.

The Little White House

Warm Springs
75 miles

From Atlanta: Take Interstate 85 south to Exit 8. Take Highway 27A south to Warm Springs.

PRESIDENT FRANKLIN D. ROOSEVELT STARES back through history from the portrait in the pine-paneled living room of the small white-frame house. The face is unsmiling, the mouth tense, the eyes direct. There is no cigarette holder clenched between grinning teeth, no wire-rimmed glasses to hide the dark oyster pouches beneath his eyes.

The face in the portrait, along with the collar of his coat, his white shirt, and red necktie, is completed. But the rest of the painting is sketchy and white. It rests unfinished on an easel just a few feet from the chair where Roosevelt was sitting on April 12, 1945, when he suffered a massive stroke and died.

The room, and the rest of the Little White House, look as if the artist and the president had simply walked away and could return at any moment to finish the painting. The leash for FDR's dog, Fala, hangs in a closet. The dog's scratch marks can be seen on the front door. FDR's 1938 Ford convertible is parked in the garage. His books line the bookshelves; his dishes are stacked in the kitchen.

From 1924 until 1945, Warm Springs was FDR's therapeutic retreat. He built the modest six-room house in 1933 while still governor of New York. He visited the area forty-one times, first to soothe his polio-stricken legs in the warm mineral springs, and later to escape the monumental pressures of a nation at war.

The house, garage, guest house, and servants' quarters are surrounded by pines, hickories, dogwoods, and azaleas. The "Walk of the States," made of rocks native to each of the fifty states, leads to a museum.

Outside the pivoting "bumper gate," built so Roosevelt could open the gate without getting out of the car, is the small town of Warm Springs. The town is still home to the Roosevelt Warm Springs Institute for Rehabilitation, founded by the president to provide therapy for people suffering from paralysis. The institute's 88-degree springs are closed to the public. The town itself has become a tourist-oriented collection of antique stores, gift shops, and restaurants.

Although the house and its surroundings have changed little since Roosevelt's death, the museum's twelve-minute film recounting FDR's Little White House days shows just how much the times have changed. Grainy black-and-white footage shows Roosevelt driving up to the gate, where he holds an impromptu press conference with a small group of reporters who write down notes while leaning on the president's car.

The museum contains FDR's personal effects, including his wheelchair, cigarette holder, walking-cane collection, and a sweater knitted by First Lady Eleanor Roosevelt. The Little White House was Franklin's retreat, not Eleanor's. She rarely accompanied him to his sanctuary in the backwoods of Georgia.

He was not, however, without companionship. As he sat for his final portrait, Roosevelt shared secretive smiles with Lucy Mercer Rutherford, his mistress of thirty years, who was seated across the room. He was looking at her, historians say, before he closed his eyes for the final time.

THE LITTLE WHITE HOUSE
Route 1, Box 10
Warm Springs, GA 31830
(706) 655-3511

HOURS: 9 A.M. to 5 P.M. daily.
ADMISSION: Adults, $4; Children 6–18, $6; Children 5 and
    younger, free.
HANDICAPPED ACCESS: Most buildings, including museum
    and house.
FOOD: Snack bar.
RESTROOMS: Yes.

Franklin D. Roosevelt State Park Pine Mountain Wild Animal Park

Pine Mountain
87 miles

From Warm Springs: Take Highway 27A south. Take State Road 190 west.

TWELVE MILES FROM ROOSEVELT'S LITTLE White House is another legacy to his presidency—the 10,000-acre Franklin D. Roosevelt State Park, the largest state park in Georgia. Many of the park's facilities—including its log cabins, swimming pool, picnic areas, hiking trails, and bridges—were built by FDR's Civilian Conservation Corps between 1933 and 1944.

Inside the rustic two-story park registration center there are exhibits by the Georgia Game and Fish Commission telling of another legacy: the coyote, an animal introduced into Georgia by "misguided" hunters who thought the coyote would give their hound dogs a better chase than native-born foxes. They did— outrunning the hounds and spreading throughout Mid-Georgia, where they preyed on livestock.

"The moral of the coyote story in Georgia," lectures the exhibit, "is that wildlife stocking and game management should be left in the hands of trained professional game biologists, rather than assumed by unqualified persons." So there.

Elsewhere in the state park are twenty-one cottages (which rent for $40 to $60 per night and require advance reservations), tent sites, camper facilities, horseback riding stables, and nearly forty miles of hiking trails. The park sits astride Pine Mountain, a 1,470-foot-high ridge that rises spectacularly, and unexpectedly, from the flat plains.

Not far from the state park is the Pine Mountain Wild Animal Park, a 550-acre attraction with a drive-through section where the animals graze uncaged, and a zoo with a monkey house, serpentarium, petting zoo, alligator pit, and barnyard. You'll see llamas, giraffes, American bison, water buffalo, black bear, elk, deer, and antelope. But no coyotes.

FRANKLIN D. ROOSEVELT STATE PARK
2970 Georgia Highway 190
Pine Mountain, GA 31822
(706) 663-4858

HOURS: June through September: Monday and Tuesday, 8 A.M. to 5 P.M.; Wednesday and Thursday, 8 A.M. to 9 P.M.; Friday, 8 A.M. to 10 P.M.; Saturday and Sunday, 8 A.M. to 9 P.M.
ADMISSION: $2 per car.
HANDICAPPED ACCESS: Park office, some cottages, and one campsite.
FOOD: No.
RESTROOMS: Yes.

PINE MOUNTAIN WILD ANIMAL PARK
1300 Oak Grove Road, Box 1141
Pine Mountain, GA 31822
(706) 663-8744

HOURS: Monday through Friday, 10 A.M. to 7 P.M.; Saturday and Sunday, 10 A.M. to 8 P.M.
ADMISSION: Adults, $10.95; Seniors 55 and older, $9.50; Children 3–9, $7.50; Children 2 and younger, free.
HANDICAPPED ACCESS: Yes.
FOOD: Snack bar.
RESTROOMS: Yes.

Columbus Historic District

Columbus
108 miles

From Atlanta: Take Interstate 85 west; take Interstate 185 south to Exit 5; take the Columbus-Manchester Expressway west to Highway 27 south; turn right on Seventh Street.

ATLANTA HAS THE COCA-COLA HEADQUAR-
ters and the Coca-Cola Museum, and Emory University was built with Coca-Cola money. But Atlanta isn't the only city with a piece of the Coca-Cola heritage.

Columbus stakes its own claim to the soft drink that conquered the world. The Victorian cottage once occupied by Dr. John Stith Pemberton, the Columbus druggist who invented Coca-Cola, is one of five historic houses that form Columbus' "Heritage Corner."

At the intersection of Broadway and Seventh Street, Heritage Corner is the axis around which the city's 26-block historic residential district revolves. The historic houses, some of which were moved to the district, span the history of Columbus since its start as a planned community in 1828.

The houses range from the primitive (an 1800s log cabin) to the posh (an 1870, two-story Victorian townhouse that serves as headquarters of the Historic Columbus Foundation). They are part of the restoration and preservation of Columbus' oldest neighborhood, whose restoration was begun in the 1960s. Today, restored Victorian cottages and townhouses line both sides of Broadway, a dogwood-festooned street divided down the middle by Salisbury Park.

The Historic Columbus Foundation conducts one-hour tours of the historic houses, and two-hour tours of other historic sites, including the 1871 Springer Opera House (where both Edwin Booth and Irving Berlin have appeared), the Columbus Iron Works (an 1853 factory converted into a convention center), and the Confederate Naval Museum.

Besides the druggist who cooked up Coca-Cola, Columbus also claims "Ma" Rainey, a 1920s gospel and blues singer whose Fifth Avenue house is listed on the National Register of Historic Places. Rainey's home is one of several African-American landmarks that have been preserved in Columbus, including the restored home of the city's first superintendent of black schools; the 1925 Liberty Theater, which entertained black residents during the days of segregation; and the St. James African Methodist Episcopal Church, with doors handcarved by slaves.

Scattered throughout the city are several other structures of historic and architectural note: the double octagonal house called the Folly; the Lion House, with Greek Revival columns and a secret underground passageway; and yet another claim to Coca-Cola fame, the birthplace of Robert F. Woodruff, who turned a druggist's soda-fountain concoction into a corporation.

HISTORIC COLUMBUS FOUNDATION
P.O. Box 5312
Columbus, GA 31906
(706) 323-7979

HOURS: Monday through Friday, 9 A.M. to 5 P.M. Heritage Corner House tours: Monday through Friday, 11 A.M. and 3 P.M.; Saturday and Sunday, 2 P.M.
ADMISSION: Adults, $3; Children 6–12, $1; Children 5 and younger, free.
HANDICAPPED ACCESS: Yes.
FOOD: No.
RESTROOMS: Yes.

Confederate
Naval Museum

Columbus
109 miles

From Atlanta: Take Interstate 85 west to Interstate 185; take Interstate 185 south to Exit 5; take the Columbus-Manchester Expressway (Highway 27A) west; take Highway 27 south to Victory Drive; take Victory Drive west; museum is immediately on the left.

IT WAS, AT BEST, A MAKESHIFT NAVY. LACKING money, shipyards, and sailors, the Confederacy relied more on innovation than resources against the larger Union navy.

Among their experiments in naval warfare were small, hand-powered semi-submarines called Davids, made from old boilers and armed with wooden kegs full of explosives used as torpedoes.

Another version of the suicidal one-man vessel, called the Viper, was equipped with a long ramming pole with explosives on the end.

Most of the Davids and Vipers were ineffective against the Union warships, but on February 17, 1864, one of them succeeded in ramming the USS *Housatonic* off Charleston, thus becoming the first submarine in U.S. history to sink an enemy ship.

Confederate Naval Museum models and exhibits tell the story of the Davids, Vipers, and other naval innovations of the South, but the centerpiece of the museum is the ruins of two Confederate warships that never saw battle. Recovered from the bottom of the Chattahoochee River in the 1960s, the remains of the CSS *Chattahoochee*—a 130-foot gunboat—and the 225-foot ironclad CSS *Jackson* are displayed beneath a concrete canopy outside the naval museum. Side by side, the charred remains of the large ships look like bones of some prehistoric creatures.

The *Chattahoochee*, in dry dock for repairs when the Civil War was about to end, was scuttled by the Confederates about ten miles south of Columbus to prevent its capture.

The *Jackson* fell to Union troops with the capture of Columbus. Cut loose and set on fire, the *Jackson* wound up drifting downstream thirty miles to a sandbar, where it formed the foundation for an island that became known as Gunboat Island.

The centennial anniversary of the Civil War prompted Columbus residents to resurrect the remains of the two ill-fated ships. A 180-foot section of the *Jackson* was recovered in 1961, followed by a 30-foot piece of the *Chattahoochee* three years later. The battleships' remains are among only a handful of Civil War vessels on display in the country. With not much of a navy to begin with, the Confederacy didn't leave behind much from the sea to see.

CONFEDERATE NAVAL MUSEUM
202 Fourth Street
Columbus, GA 31902
(706) 327-9798

HOURS: Tuesday through Friday, 10 A.M. to 5 P.M.; Saturday and Sunday, 1 P.M. to 5 P.M. Closed Monday.
ADMISSION: Free.
HANDICAPPED ACCESS: No.
FOOD: No.
RESTROOMS: Yes.

The Columbus Museum

Columbus
107 miles

From Atlanta: Take Interstate 85 south to Exit 4; take Wynnton Road west to the museum on the right.

IN THE DOWNSTAIRS LOBBY STANDS THE MU-seum's mascot: a big wooden rooster called Chicken George. It's a little bit of whimsy for an eclectic museum that includes a little bit of everything, from an entire 1939 living room moved to the museum from an Atlanta mansion to a 1900s-era African-American voodoo doll from South Carolina.

Started in 1952 as a house museum, the Columbus Museum expanded in 1989 into an $11 million, 89,000-square-foot facility that includes a regional history gallery, theaters, and American painting and sculpture exhibits. The artworks, most by southern artists, range from a 1785 portrait by Gilbert Stuart to a 1983 collage by Howard Finster, the state's most famous folk artist-minister.

An African-American folk art and crafts exhibit displays hand-carved, alligator-topped canes, quilts, paintings, and toys.

Downstairs, a children's gallery called Transformations teaches kids about the components of art with hands-on exhibits.

THE COLUMBUS MUSEUM
1251 Wynnton Road
Columbus, GA 31906
(706) 649-0713

HOURS: Tuesday through Saturday, 10 A.M. to 5 P.M.; Sunday, 1 P.M. to 5 P.M. Closed Monday.
ADMISSION: Free.
HANDICAPPED ACCESS: Yes.
FOOD: No.
RESTROOMS: Yes.

National Infantry Museum

Fort Benning
111 miles

From Atlanta: Take Interstate 85 west to Interstate 185; take Interstate 185 south to Division Road in Fort Benning; take Division Road west to Baltzell Avenue; take Baltzell Avenue north to the museum.

WAR IS UGLY: BLOOD AND GUTS AND BUILD-ings blown to bits. But at Fort Benning, the world's largest infantry training center, they've created a surprisingly attractive museum dedicated to the grunts of war—the infantrymen.

With 2,500 items (from a total collection of 21,500) spread throughout a 30,000-square-foot former base hospital, the museum includes bits and pieces of war and peace: a porthole from the USS *Maine*, a chunk of the Berlin Wall.

But it also contains tapestries, a gallery of military art, and sculptures of heroes and foes from George S. Patton to Benito Mussolini. Even the front door is adorned with a stained-glass rendition of the rifle-and-wreath infantryman's insignia—this is anything but an army man's museum dressed in olive drab.

Outside the three-story white building where soldiers once convalesced are rows of heavy artillery and tanks. Inside are the art and artifacts of war, including a jewel-encrusted baton given to Hermann Goering by Adolf Hitler and an 1890s Gatling gun that was used by the Costa Rican Army in the 1950s.

While tracing the history of the foot soldier from sixteenth-century knights to Desert Storm, the museum makes military science come alive with the unexpected. Visitors will meet Oscar, the dummy paratrooper—a hero you won't find in history books: Dur-

Housed in a former army hospital, the National Infantry Museum at Fort Benning contains an amazing 2,000-item collection of infantry art, artifacts, and artillery.

ing the D-Day invasion of Europe on June 6, 1944, hundreds of inflated rubber dummy paratroopers—equipped with flares, sound effects, and canisters of "battlefield odors"—were dropped on the Germans, who moved fifty miles away from Omaha Beach to counterattack the dummies. The ploy worked so well that 2,000 paratrooper dummies later invaded the Philippines.

NATIONAL INFANTRY MUSEUM
Fort Benning, GA 31905
(706) 545-2958

HOURS: Monday through Friday, 8 A.M. to 4:30 P.M.; Saturday and Sunday, 12:30 P.M. to 4:30 P.M.
ADMISSION: Free.
HANDICAPPED ACCESS: Yes.
FOOD: No.
RESTROOMS: Yes.

Buena Vista

137 miles

From Columbus: Take Interstate 185 south to Exit 1S; take Highway 280 south to Highway 26 east and go 15 miles to Buena Vista.

BUENA VISTA IS THE LAST PLACE YOU'D EXPECT to find Elvis Presley matchbooks, license plates, and paperweights for sale. This is an old farming community, once ruled by cotton, now living off the proceeds of pine trees, poultry, and peanuts.

But there it is, just off the courthouse square: the Elvis Presley Collection Museum, with its beige awning bearing the King's TCB (Taking Care of Business) logo. Inside the museum, and past the gift shop with the Presley matchbooks, Graceland postcards, and videotapes of bad Elvis movies, is a $2 million collection of Elvis jumpsuits, jewelry, movie trinkets, and other memorabilia.

Around the block is the National Country Music Museum, which contains the first dollar bill Presley made (certified photocopies available for $1 apiece), suits worn by the Statler Brothers, a '54 Caddy once owned by Jerry Lee Lewis, and one severely damaged 1984 Jaguar driven by Barbara Mandrell when she had a near-fatal accident.

Two doors down from the Country Music Museum is the Front Porch Music Hall, featuring gospel music performers every Sunday afternoon.

Outside of town, on Highway 41, is the Silver Moon Music Barn, a converted mobile-home factory that has attracted such country music stars as George Jones, Merle Haggard, Conway Twitty, Earl Thomas Conley, Doug Stone, and John Anderson.

All of this belongs to Mike Moon, a Buena Vista native who is trying to turn his hometown into the next Branson, Missouri.

Moon, who worked as a music promoter, timber man, and farmer before striking it rich with a line of women's clothing sold on cable television, moved his country music museum from Pigeon Forge, Tennessee, in 1992 and his Presley museum from Niagara Falls, Pennsylvania, the next year. His Moon Craft company, which makes knitted women's wear, is the second-largest employer in town, after the Cargill poultry plant. Moon has opened an outlet store next to the Presley museum and has renovated an old Ford dealership into a bar.

His biggest coup, however, has been the Silver Moon Music Barn, where name-brand country performers can be seen for as little as $5 apiece. Tickets are sold at the Country Music Museum and range in price, depending on the performer, from $5 to $25.

There are no motels or fast-food restaurants in Buena Vista, but the town has three bed-and-breakfast inns, a fish house, a pizza parlor, and an old-style drugstore with fountain drinks.

"We're just trying to build this little town up and get on the map," said Vicki Carlisle, who runs the Presley museum. "We think Elvis might do it."

ELVIS PRESLEY COLLECTION MUSEUM
NATIONAL COUNTRY MUSIC MUSEUM
SILVER MOON MUSIC BARN
FRONT PORCH MUSIC HALL
Buena Vista, GA 31803
(912) 649-2259

HOURS: Elvis Presley and Country Music museums: Monday through Saturday, 10 A.M. to 6 P.M.; Sunday, 1 P.M. to 6 P.M.; Music Barn and Music Hall: Call 1-800-531-0677 for dates and times.

ADMISSION: Elvis Presley and Country Music museums: Adults, $4.95; Seniors, $3.95; Children 6–12, $2.95; Children 5 and younger, free. Music Barn and Music Hall: Call 1-800-531-0677 for prices.

HANDICAPPED ACCESS: Yes.

FOOD: Pizza and fish restaurants in town; fast food served at the Music Barn and Music Hall.

RESTROOMS: Yes.

Pasaquan

Buena Vista
139 miles

From Buena Vista: Take Highway 41 north, go 1 mile and bear left on Highway 137; turn left at County Road 78 (the second paved road on the left): Pasaquan is one-half mile down the road on the right.

EDDIE OWENS MARTIN WAS AN ORIGINAL, A self-invented man who transformed himself from a teen-age dropout into an eccentric student of the world's lost cultures.

Dressing himself in handmade African dashikis, Martin stiffened his hair with boiled rice syrup so that it would stick up like an antenna for the voices and visions that compelled him to create a place he called Pasaquan.

A sixth-grade dropout who ran away from home at the age of fourteen to escape an abusive, alcoholic father, Martin had his first vision during a near-fatal illness while in his mid-thirties. Following instructions from the giants in his dreams, Martin renamed himself Saint EOM and created his own little world around the small frame sharecropper's house he inherited from his mother.

A character as colorful as his artwork, Martin spent thirty years filling his house and its surroundings with brightly colored totems, sculptures, and paintings that borrowed bits and pieces from the world's cultures and religions. To pay for his eccentric brand of folk art, Martin told fortunes to the carloads of people who came, by word-of-mouth, to see the fellow some called a mystic and others a madman.

The yellow frame house is practically lost behind walls with serpentine railings and mask-like faces. Pagoda-type structures served as his prayer rooms and workshops. One wall is decorated with the stylized images of the drag queens Martin met as a young

Mystic or madman, Eddie Owens Martin spent thirty years converting the grounds of a sharecropper's shack into his own world of bright colors, exotic images, and spiritual worship centers like his "dancing pit."

man in New York. There is a round, sand-filled "dancing pit" where Martin danced and sang to the beat of his homemade instruments.

The purpose of Pasaquan, said curator Gwen Martin (no relation), was to create a harmonic convergence of time and place. "This is where the past, present, and future all merge together," she said.

A hermit by nature, Martin was a self-taught artist and musician who also made his own furniture and clothing. Martin continued his work until, overcome by cancer and other illnesses, he killed himself in 1986.

After his death, the paintings, furniture, and clothing inside his house became the property of the Columbus Museum. The house and its grounds were taken over by the Martin County Historical Society.

Described by some as a "Howard Finster on LSD" and by himself as the "Bodacious Mystic Badass of Buena Vista," Martin has received belated recognition for his unique artistic visions. His folk art has found its way onto the pages of textbooks and the walls of museums in Columbus, Albany, Athens, and Atlanta.

"He'd had a hard life," said Gwen Martin, "and he just wanted his artwork respected."

PASAQUAN
c/o Marion County Historical Society
P.O. Box 427
Buena Vista, GA 31803
or
Buena Vista Chamber of Commerce
(912) 649-2842

HOURS: Saturday, 10 A.M. to 6 P.M.; Sunday, 1 P.M. to 6 P.M.
Call (912) 649-9444 for weekday tours.
ADMISSION: Adults, $5; Seniors, $3; Children younger than 12, free.
HANDICAPPED ACCESS: No.
FOOD: No, but picnicking permitted on grounds.
RESTROOMS: No.

Westville

Lumpkin
140 miles

From Columbus: Take Interstate 185 south to Exit 1; take Highway 280 south to Cusseta; take Highway 27 south to Lumpkin.

WESTVILLE IS A 140-YEAR-OLD TOWN THAT didn't exist twenty-five years ago. Started as a living history museum to house the collection of history professor and college president John Ward West, Westville (named after guess who) is evolving in the same way that the small towns of the 1800s developed. Westville's growth, however, is guided under the direction of a nonprofit foundation whose board at one time included President Jimmy Carter.

Westville's first house was moved to the fifty-eight-acre village in early 1968. It was followed by a second house, and then a blacksmith shop. Churches were added, then government buildings, and stores. A school and doctor's office came later.

There are thirty-three structures in Westville, about a third of them homes. The town has a cabinet shop, shoemaker's shop, cotton gin, county courthouse, Presbyterian church and "camp meeting" tabernacle, and houses that range from the log cabins of the earliest pioneers to the grandest house of the wealthiest merchant.

The town continues to grow, adding new buildings as funding becomes available. Its population grows, too, as it finds craftspeople and professionals to populate its sand-and-dirt streets. Although the whole town goes home when the gates close at night, during the day the residents of Westville live much like their ancestors did. Westville's blacksmith, for example, not only explains to visitors the craftsmanship of his lost art, but also hammers out hinges and other hardware for the restored buildings of the town. The cook not only makes biscuits and cornbread the old-fashioned way, but also will sell you some.

Although laid out in the square-block grid pattern of small towns, Westville's symbol is circular. The wheel is what made agricultural communities go 'round in Westville's time: water wheels, spinning wheels, cart wheels, mill wheels, grinder's wheels, wagon wheels. A town's prosperity in the 1850s could be calculated by counting its wheels.

Throughout the year, Westville celebrates the holidays as small-town Georgians would have in the past. On the Fourth of July, patriotic orators give speeches, children play games and contests, and there's an old-fashioned barbecue. In the fall, Westville holds an agricultural fair that highlights harvest-time activities such as cane grinding and syrup making.

Like any 1850s town, Westville's streets are unpaved, and the buildings unheated and (naturally) not air-conditioned. Visitors are advised to wear flat-heeled shoes and dress warmly in winter, coolly in summer. If it rains, expect to get muddy.

Just outside the white gates of Westville, the town of Lumpkin also has historic buildings open for tours, including the 1836 Bedingfield Inn, which has been restored as a museum of circa-1800 travel accommodations. There is also a 1900 drugstore museum stocked with contents from the era before convenience stores.

Maybe 140 years from now the Westvilles of the future will be re-created suburban towns of Holiday Inns, 7-Elevens, and Blockbuster Videos.

WESTVILLE
South Mulberry Street
Lumpkin, GA 31815
(912) 838-6310

HOURS: Tuesday through Saturday, 10 A.M. to 5 P.M.; Sunday, 1 P.M. to 5 P.M. Closed Monday.
ADMISSION: Adults, $6; Children, kindergarten through high school, $3; Seniors, Military, and College Students, $5.
HANDICAPPED ACCESS: Restrooms, yes. Most of homes, no.
FOOD: Sausage, biscuits, gingerbread, and lemonade.
RESTROOMS: Yes.

Providence Canyon State Park

Lumpkin
153 miles

From Atlanta: Take Interstate 85 west to Interstate 185 south to Columbus; take Exit 1 to Highway 280 south to Cusseta; take Highway 27 south to Lumpkin; take State Road 39C west eight miles to Providence Canyon.

IF EVER THERE WERE A CASE OF MAKING THE best out of something bad, here it is: a tourist attraction created by agricultural mismanagement.

More than 150 years of soil erosion have turned former cotton fields into something Georgia calls its "Little Grand Canyon." The state park, encompassing 1,100 acres, was created in 1971.

Providence Canyon, carved into multicolored gullies and canyons, is not nearly as grand as the canyon in Arizona, but it is spectacular in its own way. Instead of looking at the stratified layers of rock and soil worn down by the eons, you see a canyon that was somebody's farm not so long ago.

Erosion has gouged away at the earth to give us a view of the many layers of soil beneath our feet. Bands of red, orange, yellow, beige, and rust are stacked one on top of the other, in a 150-foot-deep rainbow of stratified soil. Hikers make their way to the floor of the canyon on a three-mile loop past beautiful wildflowers, lush green vegetation, and junky old automobiles.

The abandoned cars, some of them with trees growing through their absent windshields, were left there when the park was created as a sort of souvenir of the past and the rural customs of the people who once lived here.

"We'd have to destroy some trees to get them out of there, so we just figured it was easier to interpret them than remove them," said Don McGhee, park manager.

The park's interpretive center presents an overview of the park and the forces of man and nature that shaped it into what it is today. Picnic tables, shelters, and restrooms are available, but there are no camping facilities.

Campers can, however, tool down the road eight miles to the Florence Marina State Park, a riverside campground along the Chattahoochee River, which divides Georgia from Alabama. The park has a swimming pool, tennis courts, playground, miniature golf course, fishing pier, boat ramp, showers, laundry facilities, and a convenience store. Campsites for tents and campers rent for $10 a night; $8 for seniors. One- and two-bedroom cabins with kitchenettes range from $40 to $60 a night.

If your boat sinks, watch out—they might make a state park out of it.

PROVIDENCE CANYON STATE PARK
Route 1, P.O. Box 158
Lumpkin, GA 31815
(912) 838-6202

HOURS: April 15 to Sept. 15: Daily, 7 A.M. to 9 P.M., Sept. 16
   to April 14: Daily, 7 A.M. to 6 P.M.
ADMISSION: $2 per car. Wednesdays, free.
HANDICAPPED ACCESS: Restrooms, yes. Canyons, no.
FOOD: Vending machines.
RESTROOMS: Yes.

FLORENCE MARINA STATE PARK
Route 1, P.O. Box 36
Omaha, GA 31821
(912) 838-4244

HOURS: Daily, 8 A.M. to 5 P.M.
ADMISSION: $2 per car.
HANDICAPPED ACCESS: Restrooms, yes. Campgrounds, no.
   Two handicapped accessible cabins available.
FOOD: Convenience store.
RESTROOMS: Yes.

Macon Historic District

Macon
83 miles

*From Atlanta: Take Interstate 75 south to Interstate 16 east
to Exit 4; turn right off the exit and go to the fourth traffic
light, then turn left on Cherry Street. Follow Cherry straight
to the Terminal Station Welcome Center.*

ON JULY 30, 1864, A CANNONBALL HIT THE SIDE-
walk outside Asa Holt's home, glanced off a front porch pillar,
bounced through the front window, and rolled across the hallway
floor.

The Holt house was the only building in Macon damaged
during the Civil War, which for the most part ignored the city.
Spared the war's destruction, but also its glory, Macon nonetheless
clung to its close encounter with history and preserved not only the
Holt house—which became known forevermore as "the Cannonball
House"—but the cannonball itself.

Proudly displayed on Mrs. Asa Holt's parlor table, it was later
presented to the Macon volunteers, the ragtag assemblage of old
men and young boys who defended the city against the assault that
never came. During subsequent celebrations and holidays, the
cannonball was trotted out and paraded through the streets on the
pedestal of civic pride.

These days the cannonball rests in a dent on the hardwood
floor of the hallway. Two rooms of the house have been restored to
reflect another Macon claim to fame—the nation's first sororities.
One room is a re-creation of the 1851 birthplace of Alpha Delta Pi
and the other a replica of the place where Phi Mu began a year later.

Purchased by the United Daughters of the Confederacy, the
house contains a floor mat commemorating the 125th anniversary of
"Sherman's retreat to the sea."

A guide disguised as Georgia poet Sidney Lanier leads visitors on a tour of Lanier's hometown of Macon, including a stop at his humble birth home.

Behind the house, a small two-story servants' quarters of handmade brick has been converted into the Macon-Confederate Museum, which contains Civil War flags, banners, and other related artifacts.

The Cannonball House is one of several house museums in Macon. The museums can be toured individually or as part of Sidney's Old South Historical Tour, operated by the Macon-Bibb County Convention and Visitors Bureau.

The tour, conducted by guides in the guise of Macon-born poet Sidney Lanier or his relatives, lasts about two hours and costs $8 for adults, $4 for children three through twelve.

The tour includes the 1842 birth home of Lanier, who is best known for his poems "The Song of the Chattahoochee" and "Marshes of Glynn."

The highlight of the tour is the elaborate Hay House, called "the most modern antebellum mansion ever built." Completed in 1860, the $100,000 Hay House was the first in the city to have indoor plumbing, closets, and "air conditioning" via a circular brick breezeway that funneled cool air into the house.

Inspired by their three-year European honeymoon, William Butler Johnson and his bride spent five years building the 24-room, 18,000-square-foot mansion that incorporates a variety of architectural oddities. (The house took its name from a later owner.)

The 500-pound front doors, for example, aren't bronze but wood painted to look like metal. And the walls aren't really marble—they're just painted to look that way. One of the French doors at the end of the hallway is actually part of a wall used to disguise the elevator shaft behind it. And behind the alcove was a secret room used as . . . a linen closet.

Despite the elegance of the home's soaring ceilings, stained-glass windows, spiral staircase, and rich woodwork, the house's occupants lived their summers in the unadorned basement, where it was always 10 degrees cooler than the rest of the house.

"The Johnsons didn't want just another Greek Revival mansion like all the other rich people had," said tour guide Charles Harris. "They wanted a genuine Italian Renaissance Revival villa built so they could survive the hot, humid summers of Middle Georgia."

The tour, which also passes the town's grand 1884 opera house and other historic landmarks, originates from the city's old passenger railroad terminal, where black and white travellers once waited for their trains in separate rooms and washed their hands in segregated restrooms. The classical-style building now houses the visitor center of the Macon-Bibb County Convention and Visitors Bureau, and offices of the Georgia Power Company.

The railroad terminal Welcome Center serves as the hub for attractions that spread out from the center of town like wheel spokes. Macon's Museum of Arts & Sciences—containing a 40-million-year-old whale skeleton—and its planetarium are six miles in one direction; the Ocmulgee Indian mounds are three miles the other way; and the Rose Hill Cemetery is two miles north.

The Harriet Tubman Historical and Cultural Museum is around the corner, and construction is underway on the $6.7 million Georgia Music Hall of Fame adjacent to the Terminal Station Welcome Center. Completion is scheduled for 1995.

"We have Civil War history to African-American history to rock 'n' roll history," says tour director Marty Willett, who has compiled a tour of Macon's rock music legacy, including the spots where two Allman Brothers Band members died in separate accidents.

Willett sometimes dresses like Sidney Lanier, but beneath that 1800s-style vest beats the rock 'n' roll heart of a die-hard Allman Brothers fan.

TERMINAL STATION
Welcome Center
200 Cherry Street
P.O. Box 6354
Macon, GA 31208
(912) 743-3401

HOURS: Monday through Saturday, 9 A.M. to 5 P.M. Closed Sunday. Tours: Monday through Saturday, 10 A.M. and 2 P.M.
ADMISSION: Free.
HANDICAPPED ACCESS: Yes.
FOOD: No.
RESTROOMS: Yes.

HAY HOUSE
934 Georgia Avenue
Macon, GA 31201
(912) 742-8155

HOURS: Monday through Saturday, 10 A.M. to 5 P.M.; Sunday, 1 P.M. to 5 P.M. Last tours start at 4:30 P.M.
ADMISSION: Adults, $6; Seniors 55 and older, $5; Students, $2; Children 6–12, $1.
HANDICAPPED ACCESS: Yes.
FOOD: No.
RESTROOMS: Yes.

CANNONBALL HOUSE & CONFEDERATE MUSEUM
856 Mulberry Street
Macon, GA 31201
(912) 745-5982

HOURS: Monday through Friday, 10 A.M. to 1 P.M. and 2 P.M. to 4 P.M.; Saturday and Sunday, 1:30 P.M. to 4:30 P.M.
ADMISSION: Adults, $3; Children 12 and younger, fifty cents; Children older than 12, $1: Seniors 55 and older, $2.50.
HANDICAPPED ACCESS: No.
FOOD: No.
RESTROOMS: Yes.

SIDNEY LANIER COTTAGE
935 High Street
Macon, GA 31201
(912) 743-3851

HOURS: Monday through Friday, 9 A.M. to 1 P.M. and 2 P.M. to 4 P.M. Saturday, 9:30 A.M. to 12:30 P.M. Closed Sunday.
ADMISSION: Adults, $2.50; Children 12 and younger, fifty cents; Children older than 12, $1.
HANDICAPPED ACCESS: Yes.
FOOD: No.
RESTROOMS: Yes.

MUSEUM OF ARTS & SCIENCES/ MARK SMITH PLANETARIUM
4182 Forsyth Road
Macon, GA 31210
(912) 477-3233

HOURS: Monday through Thursday, 9 A.M. to 5 P.M.; Friday, 9 A.M. to 9 P.M.; Saturday, 9 A.M. to 5 P.M.; Sunday, 1 P.M. to 5 P.M.
ADMISSION: Adults, $2; Children 3–18, $1; Seniors 62 and older, $1; Free on Monday from 9 A.M. to 5 P.M. and Friday 5 P.M. to 9 P.M.
HANDICAPPED ACCESS: Yes.
FOOD: No.
RESTROOMS: Yes.

Harriet Tubman Historical and Cultural Museum

Macon
83 miles

From Terminal Station Welcome Center: Take Martin Luther King, Jr., Boulevard two blocks east to Walnut Street; take Walnut Street north one-half block to Tubman Museum on the left.

IN THE 1950S, WHEN ROSA PARKS AND MARTIN Luther King, Jr., were leading a boycott of the segregated buses of Montgomery, Alabama, blacks in Macon also were refusing to move to the back of the bus. They staged their own bus boycott and achieved, without the notoriety of the Montgomery movement, a place in the front row of civil rights.

"Everybody knows about Rosa Parks, but nobody knows there was a Macon bus boycott," said Harriet Tubman museum executive director Carey Pickard.

The museum is another step by Macon's black community to bring recognition to its African-American heritage and homegrown artists. Named after the "Moses" of the Underground Railroad, who led hundreds of slaves to freedom, the museum blends black culture, history, and art.

The modest two-story museum is dominated by a wall-length mural depicting African-American history from its tribal origins to such Macon-born personalities as Lena Horne, Otis Redding, and Little Richard.

One room contains African artifacts, including musical instruments that children are encouraged to pluck and pound. Another room contains an art gallery with works by regionally and nationally known black artists, such as Annie Greene, Beverly Buchanan, Ana Bel Lee, and Keith Bankston.

The museum's local history gallery contains the rocking chair of Jefferson Long, the first black congressman from Georgia, and the cornerstone of Beda-Etta College, an early black institution of higher learning in Macon.

"Our goal is to have people recognize the achievements of African-American people in terms of art and culture," Pickard said. "People can come in here and learn something, or they can just look at the pictures."

In addition to the offerings at the museum, Macon's black heritage can be found throughout the city, including a monument to Macon's only Medal of Honor recipient, Sgt. Rodney M. Davis, who died in Vietnam in 1967 by throwing himself on a grenade to protect his platoon. Davis is buried in Linwood Cemetery in the Pleasant Hill Historic District—one of the first black neighborhoods included on the National Register of Historic Places. Pleasant Hill contains the childhood homes of Little Richard and Lena Horne, as well as several historic black churches.

The steam locomotive at Benny Scott Plaza honors one of the South's first black railroad engineers, who worked for the Central of Georgia Railroad for forty-two years. A few blocks away, on Mulberry Street, another monument honors the railroad line's president, William W. Wadley.

In Macon, when an unlikely promise is made, blacks say they'll believe it when "Wadley crosses Mulberry."

HARRIET TUBMAN HISTORICAL AND
  CULTURAL MUSEUM
340 Walnut Street
Macon, GA 31201
(912) 743-8544

HOURS: Monday through Friday, 10 A.M. to 5 P.M.; Saturday,
  2 P.M. to 5 P.M. Closed Sunday.
ADMISSION: $1.
FOOD: No.
RESTROOMS: Yes.

Rose Hill Cemetery

Macon
85 miles

From the Terminal Station Welcome Center: Take Martin Luther King, Jr., Boulevard east 3 miles to Riverside Drive; take Riverside Drive north 8 blocks to the cemetery on the right.

SIDE BY SIDE, JUST AS THEY WERE ON STAGE twenty years ago, Duane Allman and Berry Oakley are buried beneath matching white granite tombstones nestled in a valley facing the Ocmulgee River.

Fans of the Allman Brothers Band, formed by Macon natives Oakley and brothers Duane and Greg Allman, wind their way along the narrow paths of the hilly, historic Rose Hill Cemetery to visit the graves of the two band members who died in separate accidents just a few miles apart.

Duane was killed on his motorcycle rounding a curve on October 29, 1971. A year later, on November 11, 1972, Oakley died in a motorcycle wreck.

Musical notes, fanciful mushrooms, and guitars are etched into the band members' tombstones. Allman's is inscribed: "I love being alive and I will be the best man I possibly can. I will take love wherever I find it. And offer it to everyone who will take it. . . . Seek knowledge from those wiser . . . and teach those who wish to learn from me."

Created in 1836, Rose Hill was designed both as a cemetery and as a public park. With its dual purpose in mind, Rose Hill was endowed with meandering paths, benches, streams, and pools to contrast with the straight lines of the tombstones. It was one of the first cemeteries to be listed on the National Register of Historic Places.

Admission to the cemetery is free, but a map of the graveyard pinpointing the graves of Allman, Oakley, and other graves of interest costs $1. The graveyard is actually a topographical history lesson, tracing in its layout the development of Macon. One section of the cemetery is devoted to the city's early Jewish settlers, another to the burial of beloved slaves, and another to Confederate soldiers.

Allman and Oakley may be the most notable celebrities in the Macon cemetery, but not necessarily its most colorful. Marked on the map are the graves of "Lt. Bobby," a dog buried in 1936 with full military honors; nine members of a family killed by an ax murderer in 1890; and John B. R. Juhan, an eight-year-old boy whose grave is topped with a fireman's hat because that's what he wanted to be when he grew up.

Many of Macon's pioneers and civic leaders are also interred in the cemetery, including Simri Rose, city councilman, newspaper editor, and designer of Rose Hill Cemetery; Georgia governor Nat E. Harris Lot; and the parents and grandparents of poet Sidney Lanier.

ROSE HILL CEMETERY
1091 Riverside Drive
Macon, GA 31201
(912) 751-9119

HOURS: Office hours: Monday through Friday, 8 A.M. to 4 P.M. Cemetery closes at sunset.
ADMISSION: Free.
HANDICAPPED ACCESS: No.
FOOD: No.
RESTROOMS: No.

Ocmulgee National Monument

Macon
85 miles

From the Terminal Station Welcome Center: Take Martin Luther King, Jr., Boulevard east to Emery Highway; take Emery Highway one mile east to the park entrance.

FROM THE TOP OF THE FORTY-FIVE-FOOT-HIGH Great Temple Mound you can see Macon rise above the treetops. It is like standing on the shoulders of the past to view the present.

The Great Temple Mound was the high-rise of its time, painstakingly built with one million basket-loads of dirt. A smaller version, the Lesser Temple Mound, squats beside it. Together they form the skyline of a civilization that occupied the area from A.D. 900 to 1100.

Known as the Mississippians, they weren't the first, nor the last, to settle along the bluffs of the Ocmulgee River. For ten thousand years people have hunted, fished, and farmed on the thousand acres that became a national monument in 1934.

A Frank Lloyd Wright-style visitor center, built in 1951, features exhibits and a twelve-minute movie that covers the site's history of habitation and abandonment.

Of all the residents, the Mississippians remained the longest and left the most lasting imprint on the land. The landscape undulates from their presence: The park is full of mounds, trenches, pits, and hills that pop up from the flat, green fields.

One of them, the Earthlodge, has been reconstructed so that you can walk inside and, behind a plate-glass shield, see how the tribe's elders sat around a bird-shaped platform with a fire pit in the center to discuss the issues of the day: war, drought, and noisy neighbors. Forty-two feet in diameter, the Earthlodge was the largest of eight mound lodges and the only one that has been preserved from the inside out.

Trails lead from the Earthlodge to the Temple Mounds, to the outline of a 1690s trading post, and to a flat-topped funeral mound once crowned by a tribal mortuary. The last Native American inhabitants of the area, the Creeks, were removed in 1839 as part of the Trail of Tears.

Park rangers recommend taking the trails to view the mounds during the spring and fall. In the hot, humid, rainy summers, they suggest following Temple Mound Drive, from which you can view the high-rise remains of a pedestrian civilization from inside your car.

OCMULGEE NATIONAL MONUMENT
1207 Emery Highway
Macon, GA 31201
(912) 752-8257

HOURS: Daily, 9 A.M. to 5 P.M.
ADMISSION: Free.
HANDICAPPED ACCESS: Yes (museum visitor center and Earthlodge).
FOOD: No.
RESTROOMS: Yes.

Museum of Aviation

Warner Robins

90 miles

From Atlanta: Take Interstate 75 south to exit 45; take State Road 247C five miles to Warner Robins Air Force Base.

HAD AMELIA EARHART NOT DISAPPEARED over the Pacific Ocean nearly fifty years ago, she might have become the Jacqueline Cochran of her day.

At the time of her death in 1980, Cochran owned more speed, altitude, and distance records than any other pilot—man or woman. The Georgia-born girl who took up flying on a dare in 1932 was the first woman to fly a bomber across the Atlantic Ocean and the first woman to break the sound barrier.

You might not find Jackie Cochran in your standard history books, but you will find her on the wall of the Georgia Aviation Hall of Fame. She's there, along with astronaut Sonny Carter and Eugene Jacques Bullard, the world's first black military pilot.

The aviation museum has everything aviation buffs want—namely lots of airplanes. More than eighty-five aircraft, from an 1896 Chanute glider replica to an experimental guided missile powered by a snowmobile engine, are on display. The helicopter that carried Robert F. Kennedy to meet the body of his assassinated brother in Washington is inside one of the museum's hangers; a "Gooney Bird" C-47 is parked outside.

An aviation museum, while honoring the thrill of flight, is naturally earthbound. The Warner Robins museum makes up for this with two thirty-minute movies that take you close to being airborne without leaving the ground. The museum's 250-seat Vista-Scope Theater features a thirty-by-forty-foot screen and wraparound sound.

Amid the museum's 100,000 square feet of exhibits are small delights even for those who aren't aviation enthusiasts. Tucked into the corner of one hanger is the first flight simulator, the Link Trainer. Edwin A. Link, Jr., a piano manufacturer in New York, built the prototype in his basement in 1929. He sold six of the trainers to the Army Air Corps in 1935 and several more to amusement parks, where children paid twenty-five cents to take the same ride as novice army aviators.

MUSEUM OF AVIATION
Robins Air Force Base
P.O. Box 2469
Warner Robins, GA 31099
(912) 926-6870

HOURS: Daily, 10 A.M. to 5 P.M.
ADMISSION: Free. Movie: Adults, $2.50; Seniors, $2; Children 4–12, $1.
HANDICAPPED ACCESS: Yes.
FOOD: Snack bar.
RESTROOMS: Yes.

Andersonville National Cemetery

Andersonville
150 miles

From Atlanta: Take Interstate 75 to Bryon, Exit 46; take State Road 49 south 35 miles to Andersonville.

IN 1865, DORENCE ATWATER WAS AN INMATE OF Andersonville, the Confederacy's largest and most notorious prisoner-of-war camp. Conditions at the camp were wretched. At one time, 32,000 men were squeezed inside a pine-log stockade built to hold 10,000 prisoners.

For shelter, they built their own "shebangs" of twigs, pine bark, and cloth. For water, they dug holes in the ground rather than drink from the putrid stream that flowed through the twenty-six-acre prison.

Of the 45,000 Union soldiers imprisoned in Andersonville during its fourteen months as a prison, 12,912 died. It was Dorence Atwater's job—as "clerk of the dead"—to record the names of the dead for Confederate prison officials. Keeping a record of his own, Atwater returned after the war with Clara Barton, founder of the American Red Cross, to mark the graves of the dead. Only 460 remained unknown.

Because of Atwater's records, visitors to the Andersonville National Historic Site can, through the use of a computer at the visitor center, discover whether they might have had a relative imprisoned at Andersonville. The computer contains the names, regiments, ranks, or, if civilians, jobs of the prisoners, whether they died in prison (and the cause of death) or were released, and the location of their graves. Visitors also can find out how many Andersonville prisoners were from their state (2,494 were from New York, one from Louisiana).

Outside the visitor center, on grounds dominated by huge magnolia and oak trees, rows of white tombstones tally up the cost of war in human lives. The graves seem to go on forever.

A two-way road leads away from the cemetery to the site of the prison. A corner of the stockade, with its fifteen-foot walls of pine logs, has been erected, but the rest of the prison has reverted to what it was before: a hilly, open field with a paltry creek running down the middle. Pairs of white posts mark the outline of the prison camp. The place was immense: 1,620 feet long and 779 feet wide. But it afforded each prisoner only a five-by-six-foot living space.

A small stone building, erected in 1901, marks the spot where, on August 9, 1864, a spring burst from the ground just as the camp was running out of fresh water. The prisoners considered it the answer to their prayers and dubbed it "Providence Spring."

The prison's commander, Capt. Henry A. Wirz, was arrested after the war, tried for war crimes, and hanged in Washington, DC. A monument to Wirz—who many contend was innocent—was erected in 1909 in the nearby town of Andersonville.

When the prison was liberated after the Civil War, the survivors were malnourished premonitions of the skeletal Jews liberated from the Nazi concentration camps. Dedicated to all prisoners of war, the Andersonville National Historic Site has been designated by Congress as a memorial to all Americans ever held captive in war. A small P.O.W. museum set off from the Andersonville prison site honors the 143,227 American soldiers who were captured since World War I, and the 17,026 who died imprisoned.

At the entrance to the cemetery is a statue of three gaunt and barefoot soldiers, draped in blankets and leaning on each other for support. The biblical inscription at the base of the statue says, "Turn you to the stronghold, ye prisoners of hope."

ANDERSONVILLE NATIONAL HISTORIC SITE
P.O. Box 85
Andersonville, GA 31711
(912) 924-0343

HOURS: Daily, 8 A.M. to 5 P.M.
ADMISSION: Free.
HANDICAPPED ACCESS: Yes.
FOOD: No.
RESTROOMS: Yes.

Americus

Americus
160 miles

From Andersonville: Take State Road 49 south 10 miles to Americus.

MIDWAY BETWEEN THE PLACE WHERE TWELVE thousand Civil War prisoners died and the place where the thirty-ninth president was born is the town in which Martin Luther King, Jr., was once jailed and Habitat for Humanity was started.

The centerpiece of Americus is the restored century-old Windsor Hotel. The three-story atrium is decorated with oak and marble, gilded mirrors, and chandeliers. In Americus, brides come to the Windsor to be photographed in front of a huge gold-framed mirror that shows both the front and back of their gowns.

The hotel's fifty-three rooms, with their twelve-foot ceilings, have been restored in period style. Rooms rent for $65 to $125 a night. Both Franklin D. Roosevelt and John Dillinger spent the night at the Windsor, but not at the same time.

A red-brick Victorian masterpiece built in 1892, the Windsor seems more suited to the coastal resorts of the robber barons than to a Mid-Georgia farming town. But although the hotel seems incongruous, it best symbolizes the town's civic preservation and restoration spirit.

A driving tour by the Sumter Historic Preservation Society takes you past an architectural cross section of the town's 160-year history, from its 1850 antebellum cottages to its Victorian-era mansions with gingerbread trim and wraparound verandas to the turn-of-the-century homes that assimilated many styles. A printed tour guide is available through the Americus-Sumter County Chamber of Commerce.

The elegantly restored red-brick Windsor Hotel is the Victorian centerpiece of Americus, a city dedicated to preserving its past.

Americus' historic homes were built during its spurts of prosperity. Martin Luther King, Jr., was imprisoned in the county seat's jail during its turbulent times of civil rights demonstrations. Like many southern towns, Americus was two places in one: black and white, separate and unequal.

While the Sumter Historic Preservation Society was preserving the affluent side of Americus, Habitat for Humanity was created to restore and rehabilitate the poor side of town. Since its founding in 1976 by Millard Fuller, Habitat for Humanity has built more than 20,000 homes for low-income people nationwide. Although the organization has spread throughout the world, it continues to pursue the goal of eliminating all substandard housing in Americus.

Habitat for Humanity's international headquarters remains in Americus, and the organization draws volunteers from throughout the country to work on homes nationwide.

The organization, a Christian-based, ecumenical ministry, welcomes visitors to its headquarters. It conducts daily walking tours of the headquarters and a nearby neighborhood of Habitat-built houses.

The birthplace of lofty ideals, Americus is also where Charles Lindbergh bought his first plane for $500 and made his first solo flight in 1923.

HABITAT FOR HUMANITY
121 Habitat Street
Americus, GA 31709

HOURS: Monday through Friday, 8 A.M. to 5 P.M.
ADMISSION: Free.
HANDICAPPED ACCESS: Yes.
FOOD: No.
RESTROOMS: Yes.

WINDSOR HOTEL
125 West Lamar Street
Americus, GA 31709
(912) 924-1555

AMERICUS-SUMTER COUNTY CHAMBER OF COMMERCE
400 West Lamar Street
P.O. Box 724
Americus, GA 31709
(912) 924-2646

Plains

Plains
170 miles

From Americus: Take Highway 280 west 10 miles to Plains.

A TRIP TO PLAINS COMPLETES THE PICTURE for anyone who has been to the Carter Presidential Library. The library recounts the events shaped by Jimmy Carter during his presidency; Plains reveals the place that shaped the man.

The Carter Library is all about the public life of Jimmy Carter; Plains is his private side. Here Jimmy and Rosalynn still live in a brick house, surrounded by the wrought-iron fence that once enclosed President Richard Nixon's Key Biscayne compound. Only here do you have the chance to catch Carter teaching Sunday school at the Maranatha Baptist Church, or to meet the people he grew up with.

The Carter Center has films of the former president discussing policy decisions and answering questions in a mock town meeting. Plains has a fifteen-minute film of Jimmy talking about the wooden bowl he carved and what he likes to eat for breakfast as he and Rosalynn conduct a tour of their house down the street.

The 1888 train depot that Carter used as his presidential campaign headquarters, now owned by the U.S. Park Service, houses Carter campaign memorabilia. But the emphasis here is the place that produced the thirty-ninth president of the United States.

"You're in a town where Jimmy Carter did it all," said park ranger Mike Jolly. "His childhood took place here. His religious upbringing is here. The campaign of '76 took place here. His whole life is here."

Just as the town left its imprint on Carter, you can see Carter's stamp on the town as well. There's the Carter Warehouse, the

Carter Worm Farm Office, and Hugh Carter's Antiques. Across the street is the famous gas station owned by Jimmy's brother, Billy.

The 1921 red-brick high school where Jimmy and Rosalynn graduated is being converted into a new visitor center. Across the street is the Baptist church where Jimmy was baptized.

The U.S. Park Service offers free walking tours of points of interest and rents a forty-minute taped driving tour for $1. A private business offers hour-long van tours, charging $5 for adults, $2.50 for kids.

The Carters' peanut warehouse no longer houses the family peanut operation, but it still sells peanuts: raw, fried, roasted, buttered, and brittled. You can also purchase, if you like, a $20 can of Billy Beer, twenty-five-cent water-stained Carter's Warehouse envelopes, authentic dirt from Billy's old gas station for $5.95, and a photograph of Jimmy kissing his mother.

If it weren't for Plains, there probably wouldn't be a Jimmy Carter. Without Jimmy Carter, there probably wouldn't be a Plains. A town of 700, Plains draws 35,000 visitors a year.

"Some are just fascinated by a small town. Some are fascinated that they can go to church with Jimmy Carter on Sunday," Jolly said.

"Some like the railroad, some like the high school. Some come just because they're Billy fans or Miss Lillian fans."

PLAINS
National Park Service
Main Street
Plains, GA 31780
(912) 824-3413

HOURS: Museum: Daily, 9 A.M. to 5 P.M.
ADMISSION: Free.
HANDICAPPED ACCESS: Yes.
FOOD: No.
RESTROOMS: Yes.

Chehaw
Wild Animal Park

Albany
190 miles

From Atlanta: Take Interstate 75 south to Exit 32 in Cordele; take Highway 300 southwest 26 miles; take State Road 32 west 2 miles; take State Road 91 south 9 miles to the park entrance on the right.

THAT DARK LUMP AT THE BASE OF A TREE IS A black bear. You can tell it's not a fuzzy rock because it moves a little now and then. The capybaras—"the world's largest living rodents"—are incognito as fat brown logs that blink. The zebra is off in the distance, blending in with the light and the shade. And the elk . . . where the heck are the elk?

"Unless one moves, you don't see it. There are times even I can't find them because it looks so natural," said Charles Marshall, park manager. "You have this big area and you don't see any critters, and that's natural."

The Chehaw Wild Animal Park proves that, given the choice and the chance, most zoo animals would rather not be seen. Spread over 293 acres—enough land to fit four Zoo Atlantas—the Chehaw Wild Animal Park gives animals the opportunity to be elusive by putting them in large, natural settings.

This is good for the animals, who are only doing what is natural—blending in with their surroundings—but not so good for the people paying to see them. If the sign says this is the world's biggest rat, you want to see a big rat.

The park recognizes this shortcoming and has plans to reduce the size of the elk pen, and commingle the bison with the elk so visitors have a better chance of seeing something behind the fences.

But the best way to approach the Chehaw Wild Animal Park is to look at it like those picture games in children's magazines, where you try to find the spoon and the rake and the rolling pin hidden inside a drawing of a playground.

Not all the animals in the park are hard to see. The elephants, for instance, have no place to hide. The bald eagles look down scornfully on visitors, occasionally squawking like rusty door hinges. The ring-tailed lemurs chase each other around their round cage like a barrel of monkeys.

Some days, the mournful cries of the peacocks ("Help! Help!") are mixed with the shouts and howls of schoolchildren playing in the park's picnic areas and playgrounds. The park has campsites, RV facilities, nature trails, and a scaled-down replica of an 1863 train that winds through the 3.2 miles of the park's pine woods on a twenty-minute tour. The train ticket costs $1 per person.

The kids are usually under control, but the peacocks are free to strut their stuff throughout the zoo and parking lot, dragging their tails around like oversized bathrobes.

CHEHAW WILD ANIMAL PARK
105 Chehaw Park Road
Albany, GA 31701
(912) 430-5275

HOURS: Tuesday through Sunday, 9 A.M. to 5 P.M. Closed Monday.
ADMISSION: Adults, $2; Children 6–11, $1; Seniors 62 and older, $1.
HANDICAPPED ACCESS: Yes.
FOOD: Snack bar, or bring your own picnic.
RESTROOMS: Yes.

Georgia Agrirama

Tifton
217 miles

From Atlanta: Take Interstate 75 south to Exit 20.

BILLY FUNDERBURKE HAS BEEN A PRESSMAN
all his adult life: forty-six years. In his lifetime, the pressroom has
evolved from bulky Linotype machines to compact computers and
laser printers.

Funderburke mastered it all: "I started out handsetting type,
and when I retired last year I was working on an Apple Macintosh."

Now he's back where he started. Bent over a table, he handsets
a block of type, smears it with ink, delicately lays a piece of paper
on top, slips it into an 1880 Whitlock flatbed printing press, screws
down the press, pulls out the type, and lifts off a newly minted
poster for the Georgia Agrirama's "Spring Frolic."

"I'm fortunate to have the chance to go back and do what I
started doing when I was young," said Funderburke, age sixty-three.
"Once you make the change to the new methods you just leave the
old behind. I never dreamed I would ever go back."

Going back is what the Agrirama is all about. Going back to
the farms of the 1870s and 1880s, back to the small turn-of-the-
century towns. The ways of the past aren't too far away for people
like Funderburke to show us how a printing press used to work, how
a sawmill ran, how mules and plows turned dirt into food, how
children learned in one-room schoolhouses, how women baked
cookies in woodfired stoves, and how an old Masonic lodge can still
smell of a different age and another time.

Opened in 1976 on ninety-five acres of land adjacent to Interstate 75, the Georgia Agrirama is a state-owned living history
museum dedicated to preserving Georgia's agricultural past. Thirty-

five structures have been moved to the site, most of them occupied by costumed interpreters who demonstrate the trades and lives of the not-so-distant past.

During the school year, children bused in for field trips wear the jeans, denim dresses, and white shirts of their 1800s-era counterparts. They attend classes in the 1890s Sandhill school with its big potbellied stove, bare plank floor, and desks with ink wells. In other parts of the Agrirama, the boys learn about plows and farm animals while the girls learn to sew.

Within sight and earshot of Interstate 75, the Agrirama's houses, farms, stores, and fields re-create the slow pace of life one hundred years ago while the traffic of today speeds by at seventy miles an hour. Sometimes it's a starting juxtaposition of time and place: A rooster crows and a truck horn blares; the buzz of a steam-driven saw competes with the ceaseless hum of the highway.

Peeking over the steeple of a primitive Baptist church—the center of life in rural Georgia—are signs for Days Inn, Amoco, and Hardee's—the centers of modern interstate travel.

In our hurry to get somewhere, sometimes we need to take a detour to see where we've been. And that's what the Agrirama is for, said Brenda Callaway, Agrirama's group tour coordinator: "We can't know where we're going until we know where we came from."

GEORGIA AGRIRAMA
P.O. Box Q
Tifton, GA 31793
(912) 386-3344

HOURS: Tuesday through Saturday, 9 A.M. to 5 P.M.; Sunday, 12:30 P.M. to 5 P.M. Closed Monday.
ADMISSION: Adults, $6; Seniors 55 and older, $5; Children 4–16, $3.
HANDICAPPED ACCESS: Yes.
FOOD: Snack bar.
RESTROOMS: Yes.

Claxton Bakery, Inc.

Claxton
220 miles

From Atlanta: Take Interstate 75 south to Macon; take Interstate 16 east to Exit 25; take Highway 25 south 11 miles to Claxton.

THE PECANS COME FROM THE GROVES OF South Georgia; the cherries from Wisconsin; the raisins, walnuts, and almonds from California; the slices of orange peel from Florida; and the pineapple from Mexico or Venezuela.

"Hawaiian pineapple becomes mushy when you cook it," explained Garland Cribbs, Claxton Bakery's accountant. "It's not suitable for fruitcake."

Fruitcake is Claxton Bakery's only business, but with a production capacity of 6.5 million pounds a year, the bakery has earned the small town of Claxton the commanding title of "Fruitcake Capital of the World."

The bakery's fruitcake production is geared toward the peak fruitcake consumption holidays: Thanksgiving and Christmas. During the bakery's peak production season, from September to December, visitors can watch the bakery's seven ovens bake forty-five tons of fruitcake every day in eleven-pound pans. Removed from the ovens, the fruitcake is cooled, then sliced into one-pound loaves and boxed in one-, two-, three-, five-, and eleven-pound cartons. In the off-season, production drops to once a week.

More than one-third of the fruitcake produced by Claxton is sold through fundraisers by civic, church, and youth groups. Only 1 percent is sold over the white countertops of the Claxton Bakery itself. The brick-shaped cakes sell for $2.25 a pound, with the most popular size being the three-pound box.

For those who don't like fruitcake, the bakery sells Claxton fruitcake T-shirts for $8 apiece.

Advertised as "baked in the deep South, according to a famous old Southern recipe," the Claxton fruitcake actually comes from an old Italian recipe belonging to G. S. Tos, who founded the bakery in 1910 and introduced the fruitcake as a sideline to bread and pastries.

Fruitcake became the bakery's mainstay in 1945, when it was purchased by Albert Parker, whose family still owns the business.

Made without preservatives, the Claxton fruitcake has a shelf life of four months, will stay fresh for a year inside a refrigerator, and reaches seeming immortality inside a freezer.

"We've had people who cleaned out their freezers and found fruitcake that had been in there for fifteen years," Cribbs said.

CLAXTON BAKERY, INC.
P.O. Box 367
Claxton, GA 30417
(912) 739-3441

HOURS: Monday through Friday, 8 A.M. to 6 P.M.; Saturday,
    8 A.M. to 5 P.M. Closed Sunday.
ADMISSION: Free.
FOOD: Fruitcake in two varieties (light and dark) and five sizes.
HANDICAPPED ACCESS: Yes.
RESTROOMS: No.

Valdosta

Valdosta
230 miles

From Atlanta: Take Interstate 75 south to Exit 5 to the visitor center.

THE TALL BRICK TOWER OF THE STRICKLAND Cotton Mill still lords over the modest frame houses on Plum Street and Baytree Place—the brick-and-mortar embodiment of King Cotton and its control over the lives of rural southerners. In the early 1900s, the mill owned the houses and virtually owned the people who lived in them, forming a self-contained community called Remerton.

The mill is closed, the workers long gone. But a bit of life remains in the mill houses that have been converted into quaint antique stores, gift shops, restaurants, and taverns.

Some of the houses have yet to make the transition from residence to business, and there are great gaps between them where other mill houses have been torn down. But within the remains is the story of Valdosta, an old and once wealthy southern city that has only recently begun to preserve and promote its past.

On River and Wells streets you can hear the pounding of hammers and the buzz of saws as old Queen Anne and Victorian homes are restored one by one in the Fairview Historic District. The downtown historic district has saved some of the elegant old mansions and churches from the city's days as a cotton trade center. The Crescent House, built in 1898, was spared from destruction in 1951 while its stately neighbors fell. The mansion, built for U.S. senator W. S. West, sports a curved front porch with thirteen columns, one for each of the thirteen colonies. The house is open Monday through Friday from 2 P.M. to 5 P.M. and charges $2 per person.

The Lowndes County Historical Society Museum contains photographs, memorabilia, and costumes from Valdosta's heyday. The museum is open Monday through Friday, 2 P.M. to 5 P.M., and Sunday, 3 P.M. to 5 P.M. The museum charges $1 (free to children and students).

The Valdosta Heritage Foundation provides a historic driving-tour brochure that takes you past twenty-six structures in the city's three historic preservation districts. The driving tour map is available at the Valdosta-Lowndes County Convention & Visitors Bureau—a good place to start a visit to Valdosta.

Like the cars that speed along Interstate 75 just a mile or so from downtown, it's easy to pass by Valdosta. But those who take the historic detour through town will find much more than the neon hotels and restaurants clustered around the interstate exits.

VALDOSTA-LOWNDES COUNTY CONVENTION &
    VISITORS BUREAU
1703 Norman Drive, Suite F
Valdosta, GA 31603
(912) 245-0513

HOURS: Monday through Friday, 9 A.M. to 5 P.M.
ADMISSION: Free.
HANDICAPPED ACCESS: Yes (Crescent House, Historical Museum, and Visitors Bureau).
FOOD: No.
RESTROOMS: No.

CHAPTER THREE

THE MOUNTAINOUS
NORTHEAST:

THE APPALACHIANS BEGIN

FOR MORE THAN 100 YEARS, RESIDENTS OF
coastal Georgia and South Carolina have retreated to these mountains to escape the heat and drink in their beauty.

These mountainous woods, with their fall colors and small
towns, remind some visitors of New England. In truth they are
distinctly Georgian; just listen for the banjo pickin' and story
tellin'. You can even go white-water rafting where *Deliverance* was
filmed. Northeast Georgia includes tributes to the power of the
human imagination. In Helen, a couple of decades ago, someone
looked at a small Georgia mountain town and decided to build a
fake Bavarian village. In Cleveland, a resident named Xavier
Roberts parlayed homely looking round-faced dolls, supposedly
born in a cabbage patch, into a fortune.

Dahlonega was the site of the nation's first gold rush. Gold
from the mines still coats the dome of the state capitol in Atlanta.
The discovery of gold here led the state of Georgia to confiscate the
Cherokees' land. About 16,000 Cherokees were forced to march
from Georgia to Oklahoma; 4,000 of them died en route on what
became known as the Trail of Tears.

More than any place in the state, perhaps, these woods were
meant to be explored. There are country stores with friendly pro-
prietors and wood stoves to warm you on a cool fall day. The
highways offer, just around the bend, panoramic vistas. The chance
to come across a roadside apple stand or an in-home country craft
shop makes every turn of the corner a pleasure.

Lake Lanier Islands Beach and Water Park

Lake Lanier Islands
45 miles

From Atlanta: Take Interstate 85 to Interstate 985 (at Exit 45, which peels off to the left.) Get off Interstate 985 at Exit 1. Turn left at the end of the ramp. Follow the signs to the water park.

THE BEACH AND WATER PARK ARE PART OF A much larger resort area, which includes a hotel, a golf course, a campground, a marina (where you can rent party boats, houseboats, and ski-boats), and more.

If you're looking for a water park alone, go to White Water. (See page 127.) For sheer thrills, there is no comparison. The water slides there are many times more numerous, and better designed, too.

The Lake Lanier Islands Beach and Water Park has eight water slides, a Kiddie Lagoon, and a wave pool. But what makes this place attractive is the variety of activities. There is a wide, white sandy beach, equipped with chairs. Your entry fee includes use of canoes, paddleboats, and sailboats. Actors perform stories from the Brothers Grimm. Miniature golf is included. You can rent ping-pong equipment or play volleyball. It is easier to park yourself on the beach and read while the kids use the water slides than it is at White Water.

LAKE LANIER ISLANDS BEACH AND WATER PARK
6950 Holiday Road
Lake Lanier Islands, GA 30518
(404) 932-7200

HOURS: Monday through Friday, 10 A.M. to 6 P.M.; Saturday and Sunday, 10 A.M. to 7 P.M. Open weekends in May and September, and daily from Memorial Day through Labor Day.

ADMISSION: Over 42 inches, $11.99; under 42 inches, $4.99; those 60 or older or 2 or younger, free.

HANDICAPPED ACCESS: Yes.

FOOD: Various concession stands offer pizza, ice cream, hot dogs, and the like.

RESTROOMS: Yes.

Helen

Helen
85 miles

From Atlanta: Go north on Interstate 85 to Exit 45 (Gainesville). Take Highway 985/365 north about 20 miles to Highway 384. Turn left. Go about 20 miles to Georgia Highway 75. Turn right. Go 3 miles to Helen.

OH, HELEN. WHAT CAN WE POSSIBLY SAY ABOUT what you have done to yourself?

This was once a quiet mountain town, sleepy but genuine. Now it is neither. About twenty years ago, somebody came up with the bright idea of turning Helen into a fake Bavarian alpine village. There are places named Heidi Motel and House of Tyrol. Employees at the visitor center wear Swiss outfits. Other townsfolk wear lederhosen. And there is no longer a genuine shingle in town: Every building is gingerbread. It has the same effect on some people as too much gingerbread of the edible variety: It makes them queasy.

But Helen's makeover achieved the desired effect. Traffic is sometimes backed up for miles as tourists try to get into this faux Bavarian village. And during the town's Oktoberfest, the second and third weeks of October? Forget it.

You *can* get a glimpse of what life in Helen used to be. It has been safely corralled into the Museum of the Hills, which is worth a visit. Using wax figures in elaborate re-creations, the museum shows life in the hills around the turn of the century: the henhouse, the outhouse, the woodshed, the drugstore, and the general store. It's narrated by a crackly voiced elderly fellow, also fake. (Funny, that the most genuine people in Helen happen to be made of wax.) At the end of the museum, as the turn-of-the-century kids are seen going to sleep, the museum segues into fairy tales, such as Hansel and Gretel, Pinocchio, and Cinderella.

The museum is on Main Street, just north of the bridge over the river, on the east side of the street.

For information on other attractions, the welcome center is in City Hall. If you are headed north, take your first right after the river onto Chattahoochee Street. City Hall will be on your left.

Helen has about two hundred shops, restaurants, and outlet stores. You can easily spend an entire day shopping.

In the summer, many people—more than two thousand on a weekend day, or about seven times the town's population—choose to spend the day tubing, instead. The Chattahoochee River runs through town, small here in the mountains, not yet the broad, lazy, powerful river that runs through Atlanta. There are tube rental outfits all along the river; you'll see them everywhere. The float through town is not too scary for children four and older (we floated a four-year-old down it), yet there are some gentle, brief rapids. The water level is higher and the ride swifter in the spring. Of course the water is colder then, too. The duration of the trips varies from outfit to outfit. Prices vary, too, from about $3 to about $6. Some companies give free tubes to children.

On a warm summer day, you're likely to find the river as crowded as a city street at rush hour. Tubing is the thing to do in Helen. From the tree-lined river, you can see Helen from a different perspective. It is still a charming little mountain town. Helen resembles a trollop who has smeared on the cosmetics in a desperate attempt to be loved. Underneath the make-up, Helen has a heart of gold.

But what make-up! Oh, Helen, Helen, Helen.

Alpine Helen Convention and Visitors Bureau
P.O. Box 730
Helen, GA 30545
(706) 878-2181

Hours: Monday through Saturday, 9 A.M. to 5 P.M.; Sunday, 10 A.M. to 4 P.M.

MUSEUM OF THE HILLS
Main Street
P.O. Box 258
Helen, GA 30545
(706) 878-3140

HOURS: May through October, 9 A.M. to 8:30 P.M. daily;
otherwise, 9:30 A.M. to 7 P.M. daily.

ADMISSION: Adults, $4; Seniors 62 and older, $3.50; Students
13 and older, $3; Children 5–12, $2; Children 4 and
younger, free.

HANDICAPPED ACCESS: Yes.

FOOD: No.

RESTROOMS: Yes.

Unicoi State Park

Helen

From Helen: Take Georgia 75 north for 1 mile. Turn right on Georgia 356. Park headquarters are 2 miles down on the right.

UNICOI STATE PARK IS BEAUTIFUL, AND IDEALLY located for those who want to explore the many delights of the mountains of Northeast Georgia. Here, you will be within easy driving distance of Helen, Clarkesville, Babyland General Hospital, Brasstown Bald, Toccoa Falls, and many other wonderful nooks, crannies, craft shops, and general stores you will discover on your own.

You can camp, in an RV, camper, or tent; you can rent one of the thirty cottages in the park; or you can stay in the lodge, which has little to distinguish it from a lovely mountain hotel.

The lodge also provides copious buffet meals: Do not stay too long, or you will be letting your belt out a couple of notches for sure. The shop in the lodge sells gorgeous handmade quilts.

For day-trippers, there are seventy picnic sites, with grills, and a half-dozen picnic shelters. Four hiking trails wind their way through the wooded mountains, including one that goes to Anna Ruby Falls, five miles away. The four tennis courts are lighted.

Unfortunately, the lake has been drained so work can be done on a spillway bridge. It will not be refilled until 1995. Swimming, boating, and fishing in the lake, obviously, are out of the question until then.

No pets are allowed in any park building.

Some seasons are quite busy. In the autumn, leaf peepers flock to the area, as well they might. The summer months are busy, too. Reservations are accepted eleven months in advance.

We should point out that forty-four state parks are speckled across Georgia. For information on the others, write to: Georgia State Parks & Historic Sites, 1352 Floyd Tower East, 205 Butler Street, SE, Atlanta, GA 30334. Or call: From the metro Atlanta area: 656-3530; from the rest of Georgia: 1-800-342-7275; from outside Georgia: 1-800-542-7275.

UNICOI STATE PARK
P.O. Box 849
Helen, GA 30545
(706) 878-2201

HOURS: Park hours, 7 A.M. to 10 P.M. Reservations and information available Monday through Friday between 9 A.M. and 4 P.M.

PRICES: Cottage rates per night, Sunday through Thursday: One bedroom, $40; two bedrooms, $50; three bedrooms, $60. Rates are $10 higher on Friday and Saturday. During June, July, and August, cottages are rented for a minimum of one week; the rest of the year the minimum is two nights.

Lodge Rates: April 1 through Nov. 30, $50 per adult. The rest of the year, the rate is $30 per adult, except for Friday and Saturday, when the rate is $40. No charge for children younger than 12 staying in the room with adult.

Campsites range from $6 to $10 per night.

HANDICAPPED ACCESS: The lodge is fully accessible.

FOOD: Yes.

RESTROOMS: Yes.

Anna Ruby Falls

Helen

Take Georgia 75 north from Helen for 1 mile. Turn right on Georgia 365. Go 1.5 miles, then turn left at the entrance to the falls. The parking area is 3.6 miles along this road.

ANNA RUBY FALLS IS TWO FALLS, ACTUALLY. Above the cliff are two streams, Curtis Creek and York Creek. Side by side, the waterfalls tumble down the rocky face of the mountain; they join at the bottom to form Smith Creek, which runs into the Chattahoochee. Side-by-side falls are rare, and these are scenic ones, tucked in the woods of the Chattahoochee National Forest.

The visitor center has a miniature museum, where kids (and adults, too!) can touch the fur of different animals. There is a small gift shop as well. In back, a porch overlooks the creek. Large trout swim below. For a quarter, you can buy food pellets to toss to them.

The walk to the falls is four-tenths of a mile along a nicely paved trail by the side of the gently cascading brook.

ANNA RUBY FALLS
Chattooga Ranger District
Burton Road
Highway 197
Clarkesville, GA 30523
(706) 754-6221

HOURS: 10 A.M. to 4 P.M, but the area sometimes opens earlier and stays open until dark.
ADMISSION: $2 parking fee.
HANDICAPPED ACCESS: Yes. The trail is steep, but it is paved.
FOOD: Vending machines.
RESTROOMS: Yes.

Clarkesville

Clarkesville
100 miles

From Helen: Go 1 mile north of Helen on Route 75. Turn right on 356 toward Unicoi State Park. When you arrive at a T intersection, turn left onto 197, and take that into Clarkesville. On the way you will pass, on your left, the Wood Duck, followed closely by the Batesville General Store, also on your left. A mile or so later, you will come to Mark of the Potter, on your right. Clarkesville is 10 miles down the road.

CLARKESVILLE, UNLIKE HELEN, FEELS NO SHAME in showing itself for what it is: a slightly dusty, very charming Georgia mountain town.

Clarkesville was chartered in 1823 and was one of the first major resort towns in Northeast Georgia. Affluent residents of Georgia and South Carolina shorelines flocked to the mountains to avoid the summer heat and malaria of the coast.

The heart of Clarkesville (and the soul) is the historic town square. Antique shops, craft stores, and bookstores abound. Browse till you drop, might be the town's motto; the spacious old stores will delight unhurried and patient treasure hunters.

Take note of the Marketplace, a showroom of fine locally made pine furniture, some of it handpainted by local artists. Stop in at the Habersham Bank's Hospitality Center. You'll be treated to coffee or a soft drink, air conditioning, and southern hospitality. You'll be allowed to select from among a bank vault-full (literally) of brochures on attractions in the area.

Bear in mind that Clarkesville tends to be closed on Sunday.

Among the area attractions we recommend: Mark of the Potter, located in an old grist mill built out over the Soque River 10 miles north of town. Inside, the building is crammed with pottery, pottery, and more pottery. Three potters work here, and the work of more than thirty artists—most of them working within one hundred miles of the store—is displayed.

A porch hangs over the river so children can enjoy the waterfall and drop food pellets to the fish, all the while lowering their risk of breaking something valuable.

Also of interest is the Wood Duck, about one mile north of the pottery store. The small shop—heated by wood in the winter and cooled by ceiling fans in the summer—features exquisitely detailed decoys. When he's in, you are welcome to watch Frank Brown carve the decoys. Frank's a big-bearded civil engineer who retired here from Atlanta years ago.

Nearby, if you're hungry, revel in the atmosphere of the Batesville General Store, which offers, the owners say, grill, groceries, gifts, gas, and gab. Satisfying breakfasts, lunches, and, in the summer, dinners are served. The owners also claim, too modestly, to sell the best biscuits in Batesville.

CLARKESVILLE HOSPITALITY CENTER
Habersham Bank
P.O. Box 5
Clarkesville, GA 30523
1-800-822-0316 or (706) 778-1000

HOURS: Monday, Tuesday, Thursday, and Friday, 9 A.M. to 5 P.M.; Wednesday and Saturday, 9 A.M. to noon.

MARK OF THE POTTER
Route 3, P.O. Box 3164
Clarkesville, GA 30523
(706) 947-3440

HOURS: 10 A.M. to 6 P.M. daily. January through March, 10 A.M. to 5 P.M. Closed Christmas.

THE WOOD DUCK
Route 1, P.O. Box 1816
Clarkesville, GA 30523
(706) 947-3032

HOURS: Monday through Saturday, 10 A.M. to 5 P.M. Sundays, noon to 6 P.M. Between Christmas and the beginning of April, open weekends only, 10 A.M. to 5 P.M.

BATESVILLE GENERAL STORE
Route 1, P.O. Box 1818
Clarkesville, GA 30523
(706) 947-3434

HOURS: Monday through Thursday, 7 A.M. to 6 P.M. Friday, 7 A.M. to 9 P.M. Saturday, 8 A.M. to 9 P.M. Sunday, 8 A.M. to 6 P.M. When the traffic wanes in the fall, dinners are eliminated and the store closes at 6 P.M. every day. Dinner service resumes in the spring, depending on traffic.

Toccoa Falls

Toccoa Falls
100 miles

From Atlanta: Go north on Interstate 85. Get off at Exit 58 (Lavonia). Take Highway 17 north, through Toccoa. Toccoa College is on the left side of the road. Stop in the radio station/visitor center for a campus map to locate the falls.

THE WATER OF TOCCOA FALLS SPLASHES straight down into a cool pool from a height of 186 feet. The pool has its own miniature sandy beach. You can roll up your pants and wade; if you have your suit, you can even swim. The wind generated by the falling water will cover you with a refreshing mist. We saw one swimmer allow the water to thunder onto his head, but he said it hammered him pretty hard.

It is a lovely, cool spot, more easily accessible than many other waterfalls. The walk in is a mere one hundred yards.

Brochures note that the falls are twenty-nine feet higher than Niagara. But this information reminds you that Niagara is impressive for its width, not its height.

The falls are located on the campus of Toccoa Falls College, a Christian school. This peaceful location was the site of a 1977 dam break that killed thirty-nine people. Your entry fee includes a book on the religious faith of the survivors. No need to feel threatened: There is no longer a dam, or even a lake, above the falls.

TOCCOA FALLS
Toccoa Falls College
Toccoa Falls, GA 30598
1-800-868-3257

HOURS: 9 A.M. until sundown.
ADMISSION: $1.
HANDICAPPED ACCESS: Yes.
FOOD: Snacks.
RESTROOMS: Yes.

Brasstown Bald

Blairsville
105 miles

From Helen: Go north on Highway 75 about 12 miles. Turn left onto Georgia Highway 180. Take that to Georgia 180 Spur. Turn right, and drive 3 miles up the mountain to the Brasstown Bald parking lot.

At 4,784 FEET ABOVE SEA LEVEL, THE SUMMIT of Brasstown Bald is the highest point in Georgia. It offers a spectacular view of the North Georgia mountains—so panoramic that the U.S. Forest Service has a fire tower here.

From the parking lot, you can either take a bus to the summit or walk up a half-mile paved path. Be warned: This is one of the steepest half-miles you're likely to walk; you gain five hundred feet in elevation. We did it with a four-year-old, though she complained bitterly all the way up. (She skipped down with such elan, however, that we feared for the skin on her nose.)

A theater at the top shows a video about the mountain, which derived its name from a mistranslation of its Cherokee name, which meant "new green place." There is a cute mountaintop museum, as well, offering information on the Trail of Tears (see Chieftains Museum, page 145), Georgia's gold rush, and the area's wildlife. An observation deck provides views in all directions.

The wildflowers in spring and the foliage in autumn are beautiful. Be aware though that summer sometimes wraps the mountains in a gauzy haze, leaving you to realize that the view would be spectacular, if only it were clearer. When it is clear, the buildings of Atlanta can be seen in one direction; the Great Smoky Mountains in another.

The mountain's weather is an anomaly—more similar to that of Massachusetts than Georgia. The temperature on the summit has *never* risen above eighty-four degrees, which is almost impossible to believe for someone who has ever spent a summer in Atlanta. In the winter, the mercury has dropped as low as twenty-seven below zero.

The difference is such that you may be ten degrees cooler at the top than you were at the parking lot. Mountain laurels near the summit bloom twenty-one days later than the same flowers a half mile below.

BRASSTOWN BALD
Brasstown Ranger District
1881 Highway 515
Blairsville, GA 30512
(706) 745-6928
Visitor Information Center (706) 896-2555

HOURS: June 1 through mid-November, 10 A.M. to 6 P.M. daily. In April and May, the mountain is open only on weekends. Closed during the winter.
ADMISSION: $1 to park. Bus ride to the top and back is $2 for adults, seventy-five cents for children younger than 12.
HANDICAPPED ACCESS: No.
FOOD: Vending machines at the parking lot.
RESTROOMS: YES.

Amicalola Falls State Park

Dawsonville
30 miles from Dahlonega

From Dahlonega: Take Highway 52 west 30 miles to the park.

THE WATERS OF AMICALOLA FALL 729 FEET IN seven cascades, making this the highest waterfall east of the Rocky Mountains. The name, appropriately enough, is Cherokee for "tumbling waters."

There are several observation decks, top and bottom, from which you can look closely at the force of the falls. Though it's a climb, it's best to start at the bottom and walk up the stairs to a deck near the middle. Stay on the path: It is dangerous to climb on the rocks. Do so, and the park rangers will deal with you harshly.

The falls are inside a state park that has a fifty-seven-room lodge, seventeen tent and trailer sites, fourteen cottages, and several playgrounds. Trout fishing is permitted, in season, and there are several hiking trails. One leads eight miles to Springer Mountain, the southern end of the 2,150-mile Appalachian Trail, which leads from here to Maine.

AMICALOLA FALLS STATE PARK
Star Route, P.O. Box 215
Dawsonville, GA 30534
(706) 265-8888

HOURS: Park: 7 A.M. to 10 P.M. Park office: 8 A.M. to 5 P.M.
PRICES: Day trip, $2 parking fee.
Cottages: One bedroom, Sunday through Thursday, $50. Friday and Saturday, $60. Two bedroom costs additional $10.
Rooms in the lodge start at $65, plus $6 for each additional adult older than 12. Between December and March, the rooms start at $55.
Tent sites are $10.
HANDICAPPED ACCESS: Yes (lodge).
FOOD: Restaurant at the lodge.
RESTROOMS: Yes.

Commerce

Commerce
60 miles

From Atlanta: Take Interstate 85 north. Get off at Exit 53, which is Highway 441. Turn right at the end of the exit ramp.

PERHAPS YOU ARE IN NORTHEAST GEORGIA TO commune with nature and escape the bustle of modern civilization. You have come to the right part of the state. But that does not mean the shopper in your family needs to suffer withdrawal. He or she can slake that thirst in the aptly named town of Commerce.

Here, not far from the serenity of Lake Hartwell and the rugged joys of Unicoi State Park, lies factory outlet heaven. Reebok, London Fog, Liz Claiborne, OshKosh B'Gosh, Van Heusen, Bass, American Tourister, Maidenform—those outlets and scores more offer prices below retail.

Then you can return to your lakeside cabin and, as the sun sets and the birds twitter, admire the day's haul.

TANGER FACTORY OUTLET CENTER
For information, call 1-800-335-4537.

HOURS: Monday through Saturday, 9 A.M. to 9 P.M.; Sunday, noon to 6 P.M.

Hart State Park
Lake Hartwell

Hartwell
98 miles

From Atlanta: Take Interstate 85 north. Get off at Exit 59 (Hartwell/Elberton). Go south on Highway 77 for about 10 miles; the road merges with Highway 51. Continue south 5 more miles into Hartwell. The road joins Highway 29 north. Take Highway 29 through town. About 3 miles outside of town you will see a sign for Hart State Park. Turn left onto Ridge Road.

STRADDLING THE GEORGIA-SOUTH CAROLINA border, Lake Hartwell is not only one of Georgia's best-kept secrets, but one of its most beautiful hideaways. Serenity, seclusion, and scenery characterize the lake, set in one of the less-developed areas of the state.

Not that it is small. The lake covers more than 55,000 acres. A number of marinas rent boats. You can fish, you can ski, you can listen to the waves lap against the shore. You won't find the crowds that besiege Lake Lanier, or even Allatoona Lake, closer to Atlanta.

It takes about two hours to drive here from Atlanta. This is not really a day trip. It takes longer than that for the quiet of Lake Hartwell to seep into your soul. But Hart State Park is a nice place to spend a weekend. You can explore areas in South Carolina, like Anderson or Greenville or Clemson. The park is also a nice place to stay if you plan to go white-water rafting on the Chattooga River (see page 100).

The park has sixty-five campsites, well-spaced and overlooking the lake. Two lakeside two-bedroom cabins sleep eight apiece and are nicely furnished with kitchens and living rooms with fireplaces.

A beach and a dock offer entry to the water.

HART STATE PARK
1515 Hart Park Road
Hartwell, GA 30643
(706) 376-8756

HOURS: The office is open from 8 A.M. to 5 P.M. Park hours are 7 A.M. to 5 P.M. Open year round, seven days a week.

PRICES: Cabins are $50 per night Sunday through Thursday, $60 on Friday and Saturday. Between Nov. 1 and April 30, the cabins are $40 per night Sunday through Thursday. Campsites are $10 per night.

HANDICAPPED ACCESS: Part of the park is accessible, as is one of the cabins.

FOOD: Snacks at the park office.

RESTROOMS: Yes.

Chattooga River White Water Rafting

Athens
120 miles

From Atlanta: Take Interstate 85 north. Get off at Exit 1 in South Carolina. Turn left at the end of the ramp onto Highway 11. Go about 10 miles, then turn right onto Highway 24 north. At the traffic light in Westminster, turn left onto Highway 76 west. Follow the signs to Long Creek, about 14 miles away, staying on highway 76. Turn right onto Academy Road, also marked by a small brown sign for Wildwater Rafting. The Chattooga outpost is 1.5 miles down on the left.

No SIGN OF HUMAN HABITATION MARS THE beauty of the Chattooga River. You see only the water, the rocks, and the hills. You hear only the roar of the rapids and the pounding of your pulse.

Well, in truth, you also hear your guide telling you how to paddle, not to mention the lady from New Orleans screaming in the seat behind you. But this is a beautiful, touching wilderness experience. If you have the ability to fall in love with a river, guard your heart.

The Chattooga is protected by law as a National Wild and Scenic River. Nothing can be built along its banks. It also happens to be where the film *Deliverance* was filmed, but no one, we promise, will make you squeal like a pig.

This is a wilderness adventure. Nobody can flip the switch and stop the ride to let you off. If it rains, you will get wet. That's what happens in the woods. Your raft may flip: it's not on rails. The crew of *Deliverance* lost a raft full of camera equipment. If you get hurt, getting you out will be a project.

That said, if you are at all tempted, we heartily recommend this trip. Wildwater Rafting has been in business since 1971, longer than any other company in the Southeast. The guides are knowledgeable and capable.

We chose a full-day trip on section IV of the river, the most difficult section. There were kids on the trip (minimum age for that section of the river is thirteen) and senior citizens. The old and the young seemed to enjoy the trip even more than the middle-aged.

After brief instruction at the outpost, you are fitted with a life jacket and a plastic hockey helmet. Then you board a bus for the river. When you arrive, you will be asked to help carry one of the rafts (and they're heavy suckers) the quarter mile to the river.

Before putting in, you will receive more detailed instructions. Pay attention. Invariably, a few people will not. Over the first rapid, a couple of people wound up swimming, and a few more wound up sitting in a heap in their guide's lap in the rear of their raft. They paid more attention after that.

Ah, yes, the first rapid. Seven Foot Falls, it's called, and for good reason. The water falls off the edge of the falls in a smooth sheet, as if it were sailing off the edge of a seven-foot-high table. Your humble co-author, sitting right up in the bow of his raft, became just a bit alarmed when he saw the cliff off which he was headed.

"Awesome!" said one of the thirteen-year-olds, as he helped fish his dad out of the drink. Indeed it was.

But don't worry. That is one of the more difficult rapids, and you soon get the hang of riding them. Holding tight with the feet while staying loose at the waist, as if riding a bronco, helps.

The trip is not one continuous ride from rapid to rapid. You park in the pools as your guide explains what will be required of you in the next section, and as you wait for other rafts in the convoy to take their turns. There are pauses, too, for swimming, for jumping off high rocks into a deep part of the river, and for lunch.

Do not forget, all the while, to enjoy the spectacular, unspoiled scenery. On your right is Georgia, on your left is South Carolina.

After lunch, you have a flat, two-mile paddle to the take-out place.

Wildwater offers other trips, as well. There are half-day trips. There is a full-day trip on a slightly gentler section of the river

To put a smile on your face—and your stomach in your throat—try rafting the rapids of the Chattooga River.

(minimum age, ten). Or you can do both sections on a two-day trip, camping near the river.

Wildwater also runs trips on the Ocoee River, near Ducktown, Tennessee. This will be the site of the 1996 Olympic white-water competition. The Ocoee is more continuously bubbly and bumpy than the Chattooga, which alternates between falls and pools. The Ocoee is also not federally protected; as a result, dozens of rafting companies do business there, and the river can get quite crowded and carnival-like. Another difference: The Chattooga is natural; the water level is higher in the spring and early summer, lower in late summer or during drought. The Ocoee is dam-controlled; the water level is constant.

The drive to the Chattooga from Atlanta is long, but if you're up well before the sun, you can go, raft, and return in a day. We did. But Wildwater has cabins, or, if you prefer, they will make reservations for you at local motels and restaurants.

You need reservations for the rafting trip. Bring tennis shoes, a bathing suit, a strap for your glasses, a towel, sunscreen, and a change of clothes. There are showers, but no soap or shampoo, so you might want to bring those, too. The shower at the end of the trip feels great.

WILDWATER, LTD.
Corporate Headquarters
550 Forston Road
Athens, GA 30606
1-800-451-9972 for reservations, which are required

HOURS: The phone is answered from 8 A.M. to 5 P.M., seven days a week, all year except for the last two weeks of December. The rafting season runs from March 1 through Oct. 31.

PRICES: The seven-hour trip described here costs $59.25 weekdays and $76.25 weekends. (You will want to spend extra for the photos taken by a kayaker who keeps zipping ahead of you, so bring a credit card.) Trip prices range from $34.75 for the half-day to $157.50 weekdays, and $183.50 weekends, for the two-day trip, which includes a steak dinner, breakfast, and two lunches.

HANDICAPPED ACCESS: No.

FOOD: No.

RESTROOMS: At the outpost.

Stone Mountain Park

Stone Mountain
16 miles

From Atlanta: Take Highway 78 east to the Stone Mountain Park exit.

THE CARVINGS ON THE MOUNTAINSIDE EVERY-one comes to see are three ninety-foot-tall Confederate heroes: Robert E. Lee, Jefferson Davis, and Stonewall Jackson. More than six million people a year come to Stone Mountain Park to stare up at the men astride their steeds in the world's largest bas-relief sculpture on the world's biggest exposed piece of granite. But other carvings on the mountain tell as much about the place as the brochures and pamphlets sold at Confederate Hall. Sloping up the western side of the 825-foot-high mountain, a 1.25-mile granite path to the top bears the indelible graffiti of the ages.

With chisels and knives, visitors to Stone Mountain have carved their own names into the rock, creating little monuments of immortality to themselves: H. C. HAYNIE 1879, W. P. SCOTT 7/4/98, CHARLIE BRANFIELD 1-25-14, DEN E. 1925, MARY ANN & GREG 12/18/79, S. O. & C. B. 1-16-81, and F. T.-D. W. REUNION 2001. A century of footsteps has worn through some of the names and dates. Swatches of gray paint have erased others. But the names and dates that remain tell of the century-old allure of the mountaintop.

Ancient civilizations left a circular stone wall on the top of the mountain. In 1838, Aaron Cloud built a 165-foot wooden observation tower, and charged the mountain's first tourists fifty cents to climb to the top—until a storm blew his tower off the mountain.

Later, the mountaintop would be a high-visibility rallying point for the Ku Klux Klan, which held giant cross burnings on the mountain in the 1920s.

These days, a skylift station, snack bar, and gift shop crown the peak of Stone Mountain. Those are scheduled to disappear, however, with the construction of an inclined railway up the side of the mountain. "We want to clean up the top of the mountain," said park spokeswoman K. Thweatt. "We would like a much more pristine environment up there."

The mountain, overlooking the skyline of Atlanta to the west, has long been a favorite place for people in love. On any day, the majority of people trekking up the mountainside are couples. At dusk, an outcropping of boulders near the top is a popular observation point for couples watching the sun set behind the concrete and glass towers of Atlanta.

The climb up the mountain is strenuous, the path winding around boulders, tree roots, and crevices: nature's Stairmaster.

If you want a fast way down—or an easier way up—there's a skylift that passes up the front of the mountain. The price of a ride is $3 for adults, $2 for children.

It doesn't cost a penny to climb up the mountain, walk along the labyrinth of hiking trails, use the picnic facilities, or watch the dazzling laser show on the side of the mountain after dark. The Confederate Hall and Memorial Plaza museums are also free, once you pay the $5 per car gate fee.

The 3,200-acre state park includes a lake, swimming beach with water slides, thirty-six holes of golf, antebellum plantation, auto museum, riverboat, wildlife trails, miniature golf course, and a railroad that encircles the mountain—all of which charge an admission fee.

A single $12.50 ticket for adults and $8.50 ticket for children will admit you to the auto museum, skylift, riverboat, wildlife trails, plantation, and railroad.

The park also includes camping facilities, a 92-room inn, a 249-room hotel, and a convention center. Because it's the site of several events for the 1996 Olympics, including bicycle racing and tennis, Stone Mountain Park is planning an extensive facelift before the world arrives at its granite doorstep.

On Friday and Saturday evenings, visitors can board an old-fashioned passenger train at Underground Atlanta for a romantic ride to Stone Mountain Village and back. The three-hour ride includes dinner, with a choice of beef, chicken, or fish entrées, and costs $35.50 per person. The train leaves the Underground's New Georgia Railroad station at 7:30 P.M.

Whether by train or car, a stop at Stone Mountain Village is worth the visit. Like something from a movie set, the town combines country-style boutiques, craft shops, quaint cafes, and small restaurants with the remnants of the original 1920s-era small town. Although the stone train depot now serves as city hall, municipal court, and police station, the drugstore still dispenses fountain drinks and the hardware store still sells hammers, nails, and bird feeders. A town gazebo sits off to the side of city hall, serving as a performance platform for local talent during community festivals. For Civil War buffs, there's an antique store specializing in Civil War weapons and memorabilia.

Main Street is home to the renowned Stone Mountain handbags. The popular leather purses were the town's main claim to fame before the Confederate Memorial was completed in 1972.

A small cemetery at the end of Main Street contains neat rows of stark white tombstones labeled "C.S."—Confederate Soldier. Long a landmark for travelers, Stone Mountain attracted the attention of Union general William T. Sherman's cavalrymen, who torched a small town at the base of the mountain on their way to Atlanta. Called New Gibraltar at the time, the town rebuilt and renamed itself the village of Stone Mountain.

STONE MOUNTAIN PARK
Box 778
Stone Mountain, GA 30086
(404) 498-5600

HOURS: Daily, 6 A.M. to midnight.
ADMISSION: $5 per car.
HANDICAPPED ACCESS: Yes.
FOOD: Five restaurants and several snack bars.
RESTROOMS: Yes.

Dahlonega

Dahlonega
55 miles

*From Atlanta: Take Highway 19/State Road 400 north; take
State Road 60 north 5 miles into town.*

IF BENJAMIN PARKS HADN'T STUBBED HIS TOE
in 1828 while hunting in the woods, North Georgia might still be
part of the Cherokee Nation. But the rock Parks tripped over was a
lump of solid gold. Its discovery touched off a gold rush that
predated the California gold discovery by twenty years. The mass
influx of prospectors led to the creation of Dahlonega, the nation's
first mining boom town. In 1835, Dahlonega had a population of
10,000—about three times its population today.

The Cherokees, however, considered the gold diggers nothing
more than trespassers. When the state of Georgia subdivided the
Indians' land into forty-acre gold lots and sold them to white settlers
in an 1832 land lottery, the Cherokees appealed to the U.S.
Supreme Court, which sided with the Indians only to be overruled
by President Andrew Jackson.

Jackson ordered the Cherokees removed to reservations in
Oklahoma in 1838, in what became known as the Trail of Tears.
The North Georgia gold rush continued until the discovery of gold
in California in 1849 sent prospectors scurrying westward.

Gold mining continued in Dahlonega even after the gold fever
subsided. Between 1838 and 1861, the U.S. branch mint in
Dahlonega coined six million dollars in gold. The site of the mint is
now part of North Georgia College, which contains a collection of
Dahlonega-minted gold coins.

In the late 1890s, the town boasted the largest, most advanced
gold mine east of the Mississippi River. The Consolidated Gold

Mine covered seven thousand acres and had about two hundred tunnels. It pulverized its ore with the 120 pistons of what is called a stamp mill. One day in May 1901, the mine recovered fifty-four pounds of gold.

In 1907, the mine went suddenly and mysteriously bankrupt. It remained abandoned until 1980, when it was resurrected by a family who had hopes of restoring it to a working gold mine. After removing four thousand tons of rock, mud, and debris, however, the owners found there was more money to be made from tourists than from the ground.

Consolidated Gold Mine tours take about forty-five minutes and are conducted by the miners who helped reclaim the mine. The tunnels are illuminated to show the veins of gold webbed throughout the quartz rock. Twisted drill bits, embedded in the rock, stick out from the tunnels like giant rusty hairpins. An original drill found in the mine has been restored to working order to give visitors an idea of the deafening racket that went into extracting gold from rock.

The most spectacular part of the mine is the 250-foot vertical shaft created by the miners as they worked upward by propping their drills on a succession of ladder-like timbers wedged between the sides of the shaft. The rock that fell down the shaft was hauled to the stamp mill by a miniature railroad of mechanized ore cars.

At its peak, the Consolidated Gold Mine employed fifteen hundred people—about two hundred of them miners who earned about ten cents a day. The lifespan of a miner in the 1800s was short. If the "widow-maker" drill didn't kill them, the dust they inhaled would.

Several places in Dahlonega, including the Consolidated mine, offer visitors a chance to pan for gold. The picturesque town has built itself around its gold-mining legacy. The town square revolves around the red brick Gold Museum, which occupies the former Lumpkin County Courthouse. The museum includes exhibits and a thirty-minute film on the history of North Georgia gold mining, with reminiscences from folks who caught the fever and never got over it.

Ringing the Gold Museum on all sides are craft and gift shops, fudge and ice cream stores, antique shops, and restaurants. The town hosts its Gold Rush Days in October, an event that draws thousands of visitors during a week of old-time festivities.

DAHLONEGA GOLD MUSEUM HISTORIC SITE
Public Square
Box 2042
Dahlonega, GA 30533
(706) 864-2257

HOURS: Monday through Saturday, 9 A.M. to 5 P.M.; Sunday, 10 A.M. to 5 P.M.
ADMISSION: Adults, $1.50; Children 6–18, seventy-five cents.
HANDICAPPED ACCESS: Yes.
FOOD: Restaurants and snack shops nearby.
RESTROOMS: Public restrooms at welcome center across the street.

CONSOLIDATED GOLD MINES
125 Consolidated Gold Mines Road
Dahlonega, GA 30533
(706) 864-8473

HOURS: Daily, 10 A.M. to 5 P.M.
ADMISSION: Adults, $7; Children 6–12, $4.
HANDICAPPED ACCESS: Gift shop and gold panning area are accessible, but the gold mine tours are not.
FOOD: Picnic area and vending machines.
RESTROOMS: Yes.

BabyLand General Hospital

Cleveland
70 miles

From Atlanta: Take Interstate 85 east to Exit 45; take Interstate 985 east to Exit 6; take Highway 129 north 25 miles to Cleveland. Turn left at the stork sign.

CAMERAS ARE POISED. THERE IS A COLLECTIVE holding-of-breath, a palpable nervousness, as the nurse assists at the delivery. "Push," pleads the crowd, urging the mother on at the suggestion of the nurse. The cameras flash, the spectators applaud, as the nurse delivers a newborn baby . . . doll, whose mother is a cabbage.

The hysteria over Cabbage Patch dolls has long since faded from the realm of Christmas fads, but the Cabbage Patch craze lives on where it all began. The pinch-faced dolls have turned the small town of Cleveland into a tourist destination that draws as many as four thousand visitors a day.

Cabbage Patch pilgrims, almost always accompanied by a small girl, visit the place where Xavier Roberts created his first adoptable doll in 1978 as if it were a shrine instead of a cleverly disguised toy store. Some are mothers young enough to have had their own Cabbage Patch dolls, who are buying second-generation Cabbage Patch babies for their children.

Inside BabyLand Hospital, a nursery full of preemie dolls is filled with recorded coos and gurgles. A nurse powders and diapers a newborn doll as visitors watch through a window. She holds the doll up to the window, and it waves a little arm at the onlookers.

In a small waiting room, a little girl sits alone, anxiously awaiting the adoption papers for her Cabbage Patch baby.

Through the use of designer genetics, some of the babies are born with the sex and eye and hair color that the adoptive child requested. These customized babies cost $150 to $400 apiece. Off-the-shelf babies, available in the gift shop, sell for considerably less, but lack the theatrics of a vegetable garden giving birth.

Cosmetic surgery is also performed at BabyLand Hospital. Old Cabbage Patch dolls can undergo something akin to a skin peel, in which the dolls come back in new-baby condition. Hair transplants also are performed, changing brunet dolls into blonds, and vice versa. Be warned: Although it's free to get into BabyLand Hospital, for anybody with small children it's hard to get out without leaving some money behind.

BABYLAND GENERAL HOSPITAL
19 Underwood Street
Cleveland, GA 30528
(706) 865-2171

HOURS: Monday through Saturday, 9 A.M. to 5 P.M.; Sunday,
  10 A.M. to 5 P.M.
ADMISSION: Free.
HANDICAPPED ACCESS: Yes.
FOOD: No.
RESTROOMS: Yes.

Chateau Elan Winery and Braselton

Braselton
30 miles

From Atlanta: Take Interstate 85 east to Exit 48. Turn left to get to the winery, or right to go to Braselton.

FROM THE INTERSTATE AT NIGHT, IT LOOKS LIKE a mirage. There in the distance, illuminated by flood lights, is a beige French chateau smack in the middle of Georgia farmland.

What looks like an illusion some called a delusion when Donald Panoz planted his first crop of grapes in the red clay soil of North Georgia in 1981. At that time, the term "fine Georgia wine" was a contradiction in terms. Moonshine, yes; wine, no.

But Panoz proved them wrong. The Chateau Elan wines have won competitions, and recognition, throughout the world. He has enlarged his grape production over the years, but also has expanded Chateau Elan from a winery to a resort featuring a spa, golf course, walking trails, horse paths, picnic areas, and residential housing spread over twenty-six hundred acres. Construction is underway for a convention center and hotel.

The sixteenth-century French-style chateau features a sidewalk cafe, wine and gift shop, and—of course—tours of the winery itself. Walking through the elegantly landscaped grounds and touring the winery with its huge white oak casks of fermenting wine, it is easy to imagine that this isn't really Georgia at all, but a little bit of France that chipped off Europe, floated across the Atlantic, and attached itself south of the Carolinas. The only thing to shatter the illusion is the deep southern drawl of the tour guide. It's still Georgia, after all.

For adults, the tours culminate in a wine-tasting session. Children are allowed on the tour, but must stay behind the wrought-iron gates of the Pavilion Wine Bar while their parents sample the winery's wares.

Like an illusion, the Chateau Elan Winery rises out of the red-clay farmland of Georgia to produce some of the nation's best wine.

During the summer, from Memorial Day to Labor Day, Chateau Elan hosts weekend music festivals featuring fifties and sixties bands. The $20 ticket price includes thirty minutes of shag-dancing lessons.

After leaving Chateau Elan, scoot to the other side of Interstate 85 and drive through Braselton, the town of 500 purchased for $20 million in 1991 by actress Kim Basinger.

It doesn't take long to see: Braselton is a one-block town. Nothing has changed since Basinger bought the town, but the actress says she has plans to turn the community into a movie studio or tourist attraction—she's just waiting for the economy to improve.

See Braselton for yourself, and then ask yourself what Basinger sees in Braselton.

CHATEAU ELAN WINERY
7000 Old Winder Highway
Braselton, GA 30517
(404) 441-9463

HOURS: Daily, 10 A.M. to 10 P.M.
ADMISSION: Free.
HANDICAPPED ACCESS: Yes.
FOOD: Two restaurants.
RESTROOMS: Yes.

Augusta

Augusta
151 miles

From Atlanta: Take Interstate 20 east to Exit 65; take State Road 28 south to downtown.

THE SECOND-OLDEST CITY IN GEORGIA (BEhind Savannah) and the state's second-largest metropolitan area (behind Atlanta), Augusta exists in the shadows of its rivals. Famous for the Masters Golf Tournament, Augusta is so often overlooked and underappreciated as a tourist destination that it calls itself "the best kept secret in the south."

Efforts are underway to change that. The city has spent $16 million since 1985 to develop its riverfront. For much of this century, the city has been separated from the Savannah River by twenty-foot levees built in the 1930s to hold back the river's periodic floods. It took an act of Congress to permit the city to cut through the levees to provide access to the river.

Since then, the city has created Riverwalk Augusta, a two-tier, four-block, brick-and-tree-lined riverfront park complete with amphitheater, playground, and benches. Plans are underway to extend it another two blocks.

The top level is wheelchair accessible from Sixth Street; the lower level, from Eighth Street.

The riverfront park stretches from Sixth Street, where a highrise condominium and shopping mall have been built, to Tenth Street, where the city's new conference center, Radisson Riverfront Hotel, and office complex are situated.

The shopping mall, called the Shoppes of Port Royal, is struggling. Near capacity when it was built two years ago, it is near empty now. The gift shops and restaurants that have opened along Riverwalk tend to cluster along the brick-paved pedestrian streets leading to the levee entrances. Coffee shops, dress stores, craft and art galleries, and a genuine British pub imported brick by brick from England are located along Eighth and Ninth streets.

At the Tenth Street end, off the top level of the Riverwalk, is the newly opened Morris Museum of Art, a $48 million collection of primarily southern art. The 2,100 works range from black painters and Civil War-era art to such contemporary pieces as Roger Brown's 1990 oil painting of Hurricane Hugo. "It's meant to be a very southern experience as well as a southern collection," said J. Richard Gruber, the museum's deputy director. "We want to bring new attention to the range and diversity of art in the south."

Centrally located at the main entrance to Riverwalk is the 1886 Cotton Exchange building that houses the city's welcome center. An architectural marvel in itself, the Cotton Exchange was saved from destruction in 1988, an effort that spurred the city's historical preservation movement. While renovating the building into a welcome center, workers removed a wall to discover the original forty-five-foot-long chalkboard used to tally the sale of cotton at a time when Augusta was a major cotton-trading center. The blackboard, still containing cotton prices dating back to the early 1900s, has been preserved behind a wall-length sheet of Plexiglas. The welcome center lobby also contains many cotton-related artifacts, including a four-hundred-pound cotton bale and the old wooden scale used to weigh it.

On Saturdays, at 10:30 A.M., trolley tours of Augusta conducted by Historic Augusta leave from the Cotton Exchange Welcome Center. Tours cost $10 for adults, $5 for children 18 and younger. Reservations must be made before 3 P.M. Friday. Call Historic Augusta Tours, (706) 724-0436.

Among the stops made on the tour is the Sacred Heart Cultural Center, a Gothic Catholic cathedral that now houses the city's arts groups and nonprofit organizations. Visitors are allowed inside to marvel at the soaring arched ceiling and more than twenty-four stained-glass windows. The church pews have been removed, leaving an expansive open floor that is used for civic affairs, conventions, and private events.

Sacred Heart is the best known of several historic Augusta churches open to the public, including Springfield Baptist Church, home to the nation's oldest independent black congregation,

From a Catholic cathedral to a cultural center: the Sacred Heart Church is the majestic home of Augusta's arts and community organizations.

founded in 1787. The church, at 114 12th Street, is open to the public on Saturdays from 9 A.M. to 2 P.M., and by appointment by calling (706) 724-1056.

The tour also passes the Old Government House, a Federal-style mansion built in 1801 to house the county government. One of the oldest structures in 257-year-old Augusta, the building is now owned by the city, which rents it for formal events, receptions, weddings, meetings, and banquets.

The trolley also passes through Augusta's historic residential districts, ranging from Olde Towne, a Victorian-era neighborhood nearly wiped out by fire in 1916, to the Summerville district, where the elite of the 1800s used to retreat from the summer heat and mosquitoes. The Laney-Walker Historic District, a predominantly black neighborhood, joined the National Register of Historic Places in 1985 and includes the home and gravesite of Lucy Laney, a former slave who opened a high school and college for blacks in 1886.

Within the historic districts, several house museums are open to the public, including Meadow Gardens, the oldest documented house in Georgia and home of George Walton, a signer of the Declaration of Independence. The Ezekiel Harris House, built in 1797 by a tobacco merchant, also is open to the public.

For those who would rather buy old things than look at them, Augusta boasts a row of antique shops along Broad Street, and the Antique Depot at Fifth and Reynolds streets has thirty antique dealers.

Running alongside the Savannah River is the historic Augusta Canal, a nine-mile waterway built in the 1800s to provide the city with drinking water and electrical power. Two textile mills still derive about a third of their power from the canal current. Sibley Mill, built in 1881, was constructed on the site of the Confederate Powder Works, the only structure commissioned and completed by the Confederacy. The only thing left of the Civil War munitions factory is its 168-foot chimney. The mill's architecture was patterned after the powder works and features a militaristic design with castle-like parapets, battlements, and ornate stair tower. Next door is the King Mill, built in 1882, which at one time housed 1,800 looms and today produces hospital textiles.

The canal itself is in the process of being converted into a recreation area, with bike, jogging, and hiking paths replacing the canal-top routes used by mules to pull barges upriver. Canoeing is allowed on the canal, but power boats are prohibited. Picnic facilities are available.

Augusta is still a city discovering itself, more than 250 years after its founding. Once walled off from the river that both created and periodically destroyed the city, Augusta has rediscovered its riverfront heritage while continuing to guard itself against the river's waters. Embedded in the breaches cut through the levees are steel I-beam slots that, in the threat of a flood, hold crane-loaded wooden gates to seal off the city from the river.

HISTORIC COTTON EXCHANGE WELCOME CENTER
32 Eighth Street
Augusta, GA 30901
(706) 724-4067

Hours: Monday through Saturday, 9 A.M. to 5 P.M.; Sunday,
    1 P.M. to 5 P.M.
Admission: Free.
Handicapped Access: Yes.
Food: No.
Restrooms: Yes.

Sacred Heart Cultural Center
1301 Greene Street
Augusta, GA 30901
(706) 826-4700

Admission: Free.
Hours: Monday through Friday, 9 A.M. to 5 P.M.
Handicapped Access: Yes.
Food: No.
Restrooms: Yes.

Morris Museum of Art
One Tenth Street
Augusta, GA 30901
(706) 724-7501

Hours: Tuesday through Saturday, 10 A.M. to 5:30 P.M.;
    Sunday, 1 P.M. to 5 P.M. Closed Monday.
Admission: Adults, $2; Seniors 65 and older, $1; Students,
    $1; Children 11 and younger, free.
Handicapped Access: Yes.
Food: No.
Restrooms: Yes.

Old Government House
423 Telfair Street
Augusta, GA 30901
(706) 821-1812

Hours: Monday through Friday, 9 A.M. to 5 P.M.
Admission: Free.
Handicapped Access: Yes.
Food: No.
Restrooms: Yes.

Buffalo Ranch Steak House and Petting Zoo

Grovetown
149 miles

From Augusta: Take Interstate 20 west to Exit 62; take Belair Road south 1 mile to Wrightsboro Road; take Wrightsboro Road west 2 miles to the Buffalo Ranch Steak House and Petting Zoo, on the left side of the road.

A WORD OF WARNING: DON'T PET DANIEL THE llama. He curls his lip and spits. Another word of warning: There is precious little you can pet at the petting ranch. The main attraction, buffalo, are well beyond petting reach behind a double line of fences. The solitary deer would rather lick your fingers than be stroked. The potbellied pigs will drag their bellies across the dirt toward the fence, but not close enough to be touched. Peacocks and chickens were never meant to be petted, and the emu, or "Australian ostrich," is nowhere to be seen. You can pet the horses, but it costs $3 a ride if you want them to wear saddles. Another tip: The brown sacks containing "buffalo food" (fifty cents each), are filled with ordinary corn.

Given those disclaimers, the Buffalo Ranch Steak House and Petting Zoo is worth a visit if you're interested in seeing a relic from the past: a genuine roadside attraction. This is what tourism was like before theme parks and airports pulled people off the backroads.

More than a quarter of a century old, the buffalo ranch added the steakhouse about fifteen years ago, making lunch the main emphasis and petting secondary. Still, there are not many places in

Georgia where you can see majestic, molting buffalo lying on the ground. Although the special of the day might be a tuna salad sandwich or chicken brisket, the restaurant does serve buffalo burgers, starting at $2.75 for a quarter pound of buffalo meat that, not so long ago, was one of the main attractions of the petting park. Dropped from the menu were the not-so-popular buffalo steaks. Not enough people were willing to pay $25 to chew on a slab of buffalo.

BUFFALO RANCH STEAK HOUSE AND PETTING ZOO
4501 Wrightsboro Road
Grovetown, GA 30813
(706) 860-0136

HOURS: Daily, 9 A.M. to 6 P.M.
ADMISSION: $2 per person; Children younger than 1, free.
HANDICAPPED ACCESS: Yes.
FOOD: Buffalo burgers, beefsteaks, sandwiches.
RESTROOMS: Yes.

CHAPTER FOUR

THE NORTHWEST MOUNTAINS:

SHERMAN'S ROUTE

NORTHWESTERN GEORGIA IS AMONG THE
most beautiful and least discovered areas of the state. People who
like mountains head for the northeast. Swimmers flock to Lake
Lanier. But the northwest has much to offer that is unique, including mountains and lakes of its own.

Two historical threads run through the area. In 1862, a group
of Union spies tried to steal a Confederate locomotive. They raced
toward Chattanooga with the stolen train's conductor in hot pur-
suit; the chase spawned at least two movies. The stolen locomotive
is displayed now in Kennesaw, whence it was stolen.

And this is the area through which Gen. William Tecumseh
Sherman fought on his way to take Atlanta. You can visit Kennesaw
Mountain Battlefield National Park near Marietta or Chickamauga
and Chattanooga National Military Park farther north. Almost
everywhere one can find mementos of the campaign: buildings in
Marietta used as headquarters by the various generals and lesser
known battle sites up the length of the railroad that runs between
Atlanta and Chattanooga.

We could not include all the significant sites. Students of Civil
War history who want to see them all should get a brochure called
"The Blue & Gray Trail," which lists more than thirty locations
of historic importance. Write to: Northwest Georgia Travel Association, P.O. Box 184, Calhoun, GA 30703-0184, or call (706)
629-3406.

Beyond the Civil War, the area holds gems that can be found nowhere else: the beautiful mountain city of Rome, which boasts the largest college campus in the world; the quaint charm of Cave Spring, with its enormous spring-fed swimming pool; Dalton, where most of the world's carpet is manufactured (and you can get a good deal); and the bizarre studio of folk artist Howard Finster, who pretty much defines the word *unique*.

Enjoy. Explore. And smile in the knowledge that you are discovering some of Georgia's most fascinating areas, far from the maddening crowd.

Historic Marietta

Marietta
20 miles

Take Interstate 75 north to exit 112. Turn west, back over the interstate (this requires staying in the left lane of a two-lane exit). Turn right onto Cobb Parkway (U.S. 41). Turn left onto Roswell Road (State Road 120). Several blocks later you will emerge in the Marietta Square.

THE BLOSSOMY PERFUME OF THE ANTEBELLUM South permeates Marietta, from the lazy, flowery town square to the elegant homes that line tree-shaded streets. The landscaped square, with gazebo, benches, and fountain, is a fine place to relax and read the Sunday paper or just to watch the bees buzz from flower to flower. Children can clamber aboard a small stationary train with a slide on the back and an engine in front. The locomotive is equipped with steering wheels and windows out of which children can lean to demand that their parents look at them instead of the newspaper. The train fascinates younger children longer than you might think; if you pretend to watch from time to time, you'll get the paper read.

The square is edged with a slew of antique shops, jewelers, restaurants and cafes with outdoor seating, and a fine theater called, appropriately enough, Theatre in the Square. Call (404) 422-8369 to see what's playing and when.

The best guide to the stores is a big sign, with map, across the street (West Park Square, it's called) on the west side of the square. (You came in along the south side, remember?) Attractions are listed on both sides of the sign. Behind the sign, a few steps back from the street, you will find the welcome center. Here you can pick up a brochure guiding you on a tour (walking or driving) of historic Marietta. This shows the locations of dozens of homes built during the 1800s, some in the white-columned Greek Revival style so closely identified with southern mansions. Another brochure describes a driving tour of Marietta's Civil War sites—including buildings used as headquarters by Union general William T. Sherman and his Confederate opponent, Joseph E. Johnston, during the battle of Kennesaw Mountain.

Also in the square, take note of the Kennesaw House, a large, rectangular brick building on the southwest corner, which now houses the Trackside Grille. This is the hotel in which James Andrews and some of his Union spies slept the night before they boarded the train they later stole. (For the full story, see Big Shanty Museum, on page 130.)

MARIETTA WELCOME CENTER
No. 4 Depot Street
Marietta, GA 30060
(404) 429-1115

HOURS: Monday through Friday, 9 A.M. to 5 P.M.; Saturday, 10 A.M. to 4 P.M.; Sunday, 1 P.M. to 4 P.M.
HANDICAPPED ACCESS: No.
FOOD: No.
RESTROOMS: Yes.

Kennesaw Mountain Battlefield National Park

Kennesaw
25 miles

From the Marietta square: Continue west on State Road 120 (Roswell Road; it turns quickly into Whitlock Avenue, and then into Dallas Highway). Turn right on Burnt Hickory Road. (If you do not care about the visitor center, you will find parking along this road.) Turn right on Old Mountain Road, and right on Stilesboro Road. The visitor center will be on your right.

Alternate part of the park (without visitor center): Continue west on State Road 120. Turn left at the sign showing to the Illinois Monument, which is part of the park. A parking lot is .7 miles down that road.

From Atlanta: Take Interstate 75 north. Get off at Exit 116 (Barrett Parkway). Follow the signs to the park.

"FOR THE FIRST TIME SINCE THE WAR BEGAN," Margaret Mitchell wrote in *Gone With the Wind*, "Atlanta could hear the sound of battle." The battle to which she referred raged twenty-two miles northeast of the city, at Kennesaw Mountain, near the town of Marietta. Gen. William Tecumseh Sherman was bearing down on Atlanta. The Confederates dug in atop the twin-peaked mountain. For two weeks the Rebels held. On a single day, June 27, 1864, as the temperature climbed toward 100 degrees, three thousand of Sherman's men were killed or wounded.

Then, however, Sherman swung his troops around to the west in a flanking maneuver, threatening to come between the Confederate army and the city they were defending. The Rebels had to fall back. Little more than two months later, Sherman took Atlanta, then embarked on his famous—infamous, folks in these parts would say—march to the sea.

The battlefield, now a national park, is the essence of serenity, though it is best visited when the mercury stays below 100. More than sixteen miles of trails provide excellent hiking or running. Fields spread like pools amid the quiet, 2,900-acre forest.

During the winter, you can drive to the top of the mountain. In the summer, free buses run from the visitor center to the summit every half hour. Look one way and see the direction from which Sherman came; look the other, and see the skyline of the city that was his target.

Or hike through the park and see miles of earthworks behind which both Confederate and Union soldiers hid and died. Relic hunting is prohibited. Possession of a metal detector in the park is against the law.

The visitor center houses a Civil War bookstore and a small museum, and offers a ten-minute slide show on the Atlanta campaign. Maps of the trails and mileage charts are free. In front of the center, near several of the cannon that dot the park, Civil War re-enactments often take place.

KENNESAW MOUNTAIN BATTLEFIELD NATIONAL PARK
Superintendent
900 Kennesaw Mountain Drive
Kennesaw, GA 30144
(404) 427-4686

HOURS: 8:30 A.M. to 5 P.M. weekdays; 8:30 A.M. to 6 P.M. weekends.

ADMISSION: Free.

HANDICAPPED ACCESS: The visitor center is accessible; so are some, but by no means all, of the trails. Handicapped visitors can drive to the summit if they notify park officials and follow the shuttle bus.

FOOD: No.

RESTROOMS: At the visitor center.

White Water and American Adventures

Marietta
20 miles

From Atlanta: Take Interstate 75 north. Get off at Exit 113.
Go west on North Marietta Parkway, back over the inter-
state. Turn left onto North Cobb Parkway. The parks will be
on your left.

TRUE, THE TWO AMUSEMENT PARKS SHARE A parking lot. You can buy one ticket that gets you into both. But abandon the idea that you'll do one in the morning and the other in the afternoon. Either is usually enough to fatigue the most indefatigable traveler. Pick one.

White Water

IF THE PHRASE "VARIATIONS ON A THEME" holds meaning for you, then you can begin to understand White Water. How many ways can there be, after all, to build a water slide? The answer turns out to be quite a few indeed. You will find forty or so variations on this seemingly simple theme at this scenic and well-run park.

You can slide fast or slow, straight or curvy, in the sunlight or through a tunnel. You can slide on your back, on a one-person tube, on a two-person tube, or on a five-person raft. All slides are rated according to how hair-raising they are. "Relaxing," to our way of thinking, means boring. A four-year-old we took enjoyed some of the "thrilling" slides. "Aggressive" rides start to stand your hair on end. Most exciting is the Dragon's Tail, in which the slider becomes airborne. (The scariest part, actually, is launching yourself after having listened in line to a dozen repetitions of a taped message warning you to turn back now if you have ever had back or heart problems.)

White Water also features two well-equipped kiddie pools in which toddlers can have fun for hours. A large wave pool is called, of course, the Atlanta Ocean.

All of this is nicely tucked among thousands of trees, which give the park a relaxing, country air. You'd never guess you were hard by the interstate in one of the country's major metropolitan areas.

Beach chairs are available. Lockers can be rented. It's best to find a chair and set up a home base while roaming from slide to slide.

You must wear a bathing suit to slide; shorts or other imitations are not allowed. You may wear glasses on any ride, including Dragon's Tail, but they must be strapped onto your head.

One more tip: If you have a choice, go during the week. Like Disney World, White Water moves crowds efficiently. But during the summer months, you'll find it plenty crowded even on weekdays.

WHITE WATER
250 North Cobb Parkway
Marietta, GA 30062
(404) 424-9283

HOURS: 10 A.M. to 6 P.M. the first four weekends in May. Open daily from Memorial Day through Labor Day; hours vary during peak season, so call for information.

ADMISSION: $17.99 plus tax. Children under 4 feet tall, $10.99 plus tax; Children younger than 3, free; Adults 62 and older, free. (Admission to White Water and American Adventures both is $19.99 for adults and $15.99 for children.) Parking costs $2 per car.

HANDICAPPED ACCESS: The park is, but the slides are not.
FOOD: Yes.
RESTROOMS: Yes.

American Adventures

UNLIKE WHITE WATER, WHICH WILL ENTERTAIN people of all ages, American Adventures is geared toward the prepubescent set. It will bore teens stiff, but it will delight children younger than ten or twelve. And why not? It is an entire amusement park built just for them.

The rides here churn the stomach but do not terrify. There are tree-top swings, a Tilt-a-Whirl, bumper cars, and a tame roller coaster. There are rides for toddlers, too—a train that diapered engineers can pretend to drive around the tracks and airplanes that go neither high nor fast.

The price of admission gets kids as many rides as they want, so there is no haggling over buying more tickets. Adventurous little ones can ride until they are green around the gills. The one exception is the go-cart race—one admission buys only one race, which is a pity, because it is the ride adults most enjoy. (Adults can drive kids who need help.)

Indoors, there are a carousel, a playroom, and a restaurant.

AMERICAN ADVENTURES
250 North Cobb Parkway
Marietta, GA 30062
(404) 424-9283

HOURS: The park is open year-round. Hours change seasonally; call for information.

ADMISSION: $10.99. Parents ride free with children who need assistance, or they can pay $4.99 for a parent pass good for all rides.

HANDICAPPED ACCESS: The park is, but the rides are not.

FOOD: Yes.

RESTROOMS: Yes.

Big Shanty Museum

Kennesaw
25 miles

From Atlanta: Take Interstate 75 north. Get off at Exit 118.
Go west (back across the interstate) on Cherokee Street.
After 2 miles, you will see the museum on the right.

BIG SHANTY MUSEUM HOUSES THE LOCO-
motive stolen by Union spies in a 1962 Civil War episode reminis-
cent of the Keystone Kops. The affair did not influence the outcome
of the war, but it did spawn two movies: *The General,* a 1926 silent
starring Buster Keaton; and *The Great Locomotive Chase,* a 1956
Disney movie starring Fess Parker.

The stolen locomotive, the General, gleams grandly in the
center of this small museum amid assorted Civil War memorabilia.
Every half hour, a videotape tells the story of the raid led by Union
spy James J. Andrews. The tape is blurry enough that it nearly
obscures the excitement of the chase—but not quite.

It is more fun to see the General when you know the story, so
let us help. On April 7, 1862, Andrews left Shelbyville, Tennessee,
leading twenty-three volunteers dressed in civilian clothes. Their
cover story was that they were Yankee-hating Kentuckians moving
south to join the Confederate army.

Their real goal was to catch a train to Marietta, steal a train,
and race northward back toward Chattanooga, burning railway
bridges behind them. From Chattanooga, they would ride the train
westward and meet a Union division led by Brig. Gen. Ormsby
MacKnight Mitchell, which would have worked its way from Tennessee into northern Alabama. Chattanooga would then be cut off
from Confederate reinforcement, and Mitchell could capture it.

At the start, rain set the Union spies back a day. The delay
would prove fatal, because General Mitchell was still on schedule.

The spies made it to Marietta. Some of them slept in the Kennesaw House hotel, which now houses the Trackside Grill (see Historic Marietta, page 123). The next morning, April 12, the men met in Andrews' hotel room for a final briefing, then boarded the northbound train. Its locomotive was the General.

In the town of Big Shanty, now Kennesaw, everyone left the train for breakfast at a hotel 100 yards from where the museum now stands. The raiders quietly uncoupled most of the train, climbed aboard, and chugged away.

The conductor, William Fuller, took off after the train on foot. Then he commandeered a repair crew's small handcar and chased the General by poling himself along. Twice, he was thrown off the tracks where Andrews' men had uprooted the rails. Then he met a southbound freight train pulled by a locomotive called the Texas— the same kind of engine as the General.

The chase was on. Fuller chugged furiously up the track in reverse. Andrews' men tore up rails and dropped crossties behind them to slow the pursuers. But Fuller was relentless. The Andrews men uncoupled the few cars they were still towing, to obstruct the track. Fuller, pushing the cars ahead of him, kept coming.

The Andrews men had to stop to take on wood and water. More importantly, they kept having to pull off and wait for southbound trains to pass. The Confederates in Chattanooga, alerted to trouble by the movement of General Mitchell, were shipping supplies out of Chattanooga. Had Andrews been on schedule, instead of a day late, he would have had no such delays—and he would have succeeded.

As it was, the General ran out of wood and ground to a halt. Andrews' raiders fled into the woods a mile south of the Tennessee border, but were soon captured.

Eight, including Andrews, were hanged a block from Peachtree Street in Atlanta. Another eight escaped. Some jumped into the Chattahoochee River and so made their way to Union forces in the Gulf of Mexico. Others were exchanged in 1863 for Confederate prisoners. The survivors were the first recipients of the Congressional Medal of Honor.

The General served the Confederacy for the remainder of the war.

BIG SHANTY MUSEUM
2829 Cherokee Street
Kennesaw, GA 30144
(404) 427-2117

HOURS: Monday through Saturday, 9:30 A.M. to 5:30 P.M. On
Sundays, and during December, January, and February,
noon to 5:30 P.M. Closed on Easter, Thanksgiving, Christmas, and New Year's.

ADMISSION: Adults, $2.50; Seniors 65 and older, $2; Children
7–15, $1; Children 6 and younger, free.

HANDICAPPED ACCESS: Partially. The area around the General, yes. The upstairs room, in which a videotape about the
chase is shown, no.

FOOD: No.

RESTROOMS: Yes.

Allatoona Lake

30 miles

ALLATOONA LAKE INCLUDES 12,000 ACRES OF water and 270 miles of shoreline. We cannot describe here all the places to boat, fish, swim, camp, and ski. If you like to explore, you will doubtless come across small, secluded coves few others have discovered.

We can tell you that the lake is scenic. It pools its way among the hills, each of the lake's many arms not even hinting at the size of the whole. The piney woods reach to the water's edge. It is less well known than Lake Lanier, perhaps because it is smaller, which is to your advantage. While many Atlantans escape the summer heat by rushing en masse to Lanier, you can cool yourself in the more tranquil waters of Allatoona.

You can find along the shore facilities run by the state, by the U.S. Army Corps of Engineers, and by private owners. We include a description of one of each type that we have visited and found to be pleasant.

Buckhead Beach Club
Cartersville
30 miles

From Atlanta: Take Interstate 75 north. Get off at Exit 122. Go east 1.5 miles until you reach Allatoona Landing Marina; you will see signs for the beach.

THIS IS A NICE BEACH FOR A PLACE DUE SOUTH of Detroit and 250 miles from the nearest ocean. It curves—wide, sandy, and horseshoe-shaped—along a sheltered cove. A dock floats about twenty-five yards off shore. Just beyond that sits a tiny island, which protects the beach from the wake of ski boats. If you walk on the island, beware of the duck poop. It's plentiful.

On shore, a cabana sells drinks. Picnic tables and grills are located in the shade of nearby pines. We visited on a 98-degree holiday, yet the beach was not crowded. A nice place to spend a day.

BUCKHEAD BEACH CLUB
24 Allatoona Landing Road
Cartersville, GA 30120
(404) 917-1147

HOURS: Open seven days a week between Memorial Day and Labor Day. Monday through Thursday, 10:30 A.M. to 5 P.M.; Friday and Saturday, 10:30 A.M. to 10 P.M.; Sunday, 10:30 A.M. to 6 P.M.
ADMISSION: Adults, $2.50; Children 6–12, $1.50; Children younger than 6, free.
HANDICAPPED ACCESS: Yes.
FOOD: Yes.
RESTROOMS: Yes, with changing booths and showers.

Red Top Mountain State Park
Cartersville
30 miles

From Atlanta: Take Interstate 75 north. Get off at Exit 123. Turn right at the end of the ramp. This road leads straight into the park.

IF, INSTEAD OF A DAY AT THE BEACH, YOU SEEK a full-blown lakeside camping experience, we recommend Red Top Mountain State Park. It is beautiful, woodsy, rife with deer, and offers boating, skiing, swimming, tennis, cottages, campsites for tents and trailers, and a hotel-like lodge with a restaurant and a swimming pool.

It provides, in short, 1,950 well-maintained acres of quiet lakeside, get-away-from-it-all forest camping a mere thirty miles from metro Atlanta.

RED TOP MOUNTAIN STATE PARK & LODGE
781 Red Top Mountain Road, SE
Cartersville, GA 30120
Park: (404) 975-4203
Lodge: (404) 975-4222

HOURS: Park: 7 A.M. to 10 P.M. Park office: 8 A.M. to 5 P.M.,
  Monday through Friday.
PRICES: Day use requires a $2 park pass. Lodge: Dec. 1 through
  March 31, $40 for one adult; April 1 through Nov. 30, $45
  for one adult; Children 12 and younger in the same room as
  adult, free.
    Two-bedroom cottages are $50 Sunday through Thursday,
  $60 on Friday and Saturday. There is a $10 discount for
  seniors 62 and older, and a $10 discount Sunday through
  Thursday between Dec. 1 and March 31.
    Camping is $10 per night.
HANDICAPPED ACCESS: Yes.
FOOD: Restaurant in the hotel.
RESTROOMS: Yes.

Old Highway 41
Number 3 Campground
Cartersville
45 miles

*From Atlanta: Take Interstate 75 north. Get off at Exit 122
(Glade Road). At the first traffic light, turn right onto Highway 92. Go straight about 2 miles, over a bridge, then turn
left down onto a ramp to Route 293. Turn left again under
the bridge onto 293. About 3 miles down the road you will
see a sign for the campground on the right.*

THE NUMBER THREE CAMPGROUND, RUN BY
the U.S. Army Corps of Engineers, has well-spaced tent and trailer
sites overlooking the lake. (The folks in the corps run a nice
campground, but they're none too snappy with the names.) This is

a good place to go if you want a quieter camping experience in a place smaller (much) and less well-known than the state park.

The park has a beach, playground, washer and dryer, and boat launching ramp. Reservations are not accepted.

OLD HIGHWAY 41 NUMBER THREE CAMPGROUND
Army Corps of Engineers
Resource Manager's Office
P.O. Box 487
Cartersville, GA 30102
(404) 688-7870

HOURS: 7 A.M. to 11 P.M.
PRICES: $10, $12 with electricity.
HANDICAPPED ACCESS: No.
FOOD: No.
RESTROOMS: Yes.

The Etowah Indian mounds, used as burial places by Mississippian Indians who disappeared from this area before the Cherokee arrived, offer a history lesson and a view of the surrounding countryside.

Etowah Indian Mounds

Cartersville
45 miles

*From Atlanta: Take Interstate 75 north. Get off at Exit 124.
Turn left at the end of the ramp. Follow the brown signs to
the Etowah Indian Mounds.*

IT IS EASY TO THINK THIS AREA'S RICH HISTORY
began and ended with the Civil War. But one thousand years ago,
before this land was settled by Europeans, even before it was home
to the Cherokee, Mississippian Indians lived here.

The Etowah Indian Mounds are what remains of a Mississippian city—four tall, flat-topped pyramids in which the dead were
buried in elaborate costumes. This is considered the most intact
Mississippian site in the Southeast.

Staircases up the sides of the mounds allow visitors to climb to
the top to enjoy the view. A small museum houses Native American
artifacts, pictures of what the village looked like, and a replica of a
Mississippian gravesite. A short film about the natives is shown
continually.

Along the banks of the Etowah River are benches where a
quiet picnic lunch can be enjoyed.

ETOWAH INDIAN MOUNDS STATE HISTORIC SITE
813 Indian Mounds Road, SW
Cartersville, GA 30120
(404) 387-3747

HOURS: Tuesday through Saturday, 9 A.M. to 5 P.M.; Sunday,
2 P.M. to 5:30 P.M. Closed Mondays, with the exception of
some legal holidays.
ADMISSION: Adults, $2; Youths 6–18, $1; Children younger
than 6, free.
HANDICAPPED ACCESS: The museum and the area around the
mounds are accessible; the mounds are not.
FOOD: No.
RESTROOMS: Yes.

These Indian sculptures are among the artifacts remaining from a civilization that populated Georgia 1,000 years ago.

Rome

Rome
65 miles

From Atlanta: Take Interstate 75 north. Get off at Exit 125 (Rome). At the bottom of the ramp, turn left. Go 2.3 miles to the T intersection. Turn left, then make an immediate right onto Highway 41. Go 2.7 miles. Bear right onto U.S. 411. It is 23 miles to Rome. Take 27 north into the city; the visitor center, a little yellow depot, sits on a hill opposite the Days Inn.

ROME, GEORGIA, MAY BE BUILT AROUND SEVEN hills, but no one would mistake this delightful mountain city of 30,000 residents for the capital of Italy.

It is, nonetheless, well worth a visit. Rome has a charming historic district, an impressive Native American heritage, and a rather graphic statue that was a gift from Rome, Italy—by order of the facist dictator Benito Mussolini.

But it is the "Miracle in the Mountains"—the story of how Martha Berry founded a respected college in this most unlikely of places—that draws visitors from around the world. Rome is also within half an hour of the quaint, antique-filled town of Cave Spring, and the bizarre, almost phantasmagoric art garden of the religious folk painter Howard Finster.

Historic Rome

YOU CAN OBTAIN FROM THE CONVENTION & Visitors Bureau a cassette tape to plug into your car stereo to guide you as you drive through Rome's historic area.

Rome's clock tower was built in 1871 atop a foundry that had manufactured cannon for the Confederacy, and which was destroyed by Union troops during the Civil War.

Downtown Rome is built where the Oostanula and Etowah rivers converge to form the Coosa, which flows into the Gulf of Mexico. Broad Street is the heart of downtown, and the northern border of the richest part of the historic district.

In front of City Hall you will see the *Capitoline Wolf*, the statue given to Rome by Mussolini in 1929. The statue depicts the early life of the twins Romulus and Remus, who were supposed to have been tossed to their deaths in the river Tiber. They were saved, however, and nursed by a she-wolf until discovered by a shepherd. They grew up; Romulus slew Remus, then built Rome, which draws its name from his. The statue shows the twin babies, mouths agape beneath the swollen teats of the wolf who suckled them as infants.

Beautiful historic homes line the streets south of Broad. Try Second Avenue or Fourth Avenue, or let the cassette be your guide.

Also of interest is Rome's Clock Tower, built as a water tower in 1871 atop a foundry that had manufactured cannon for the Confederacy—and which was, naturally, destroyed by Gen. William T. Sherman on his way from Chattanooga to Atlanta.

GREATER ROME CONVENTION & VISITORS BUREAU
410 Civic Hall
Mailing Address: P.O. Box 5823
Rome, GA 30162-5823
(706) 295-5576; 1-800-444-1834

HOURS: Monday through Friday, 9 A.M. to 5 P.M.; Saturday, 10 A.M. to 3 P.M.; Sunday, noon to 3 P.M.
ADMISSION: Free. The guide cassette costs $5 if you want to keep it, but they will lend it to you for free.
HANDICAPPED ACCESS: Visitor center, No.
FOOD: No.
RESTROOMS: Yes.

The Miracle in the Mountains: The Martha Berry Museum, Oak Hill, and Berry College

Rome
65 miles

To the museum and the Oak Hill plantation: Continue past the visitor center on Rtes. 27, 20, and U.S. 1 (Also called Turner McCall Boulevard). Turn to the right to stay on Highway 27. Go about 5 miles to Georgia Loop 1. Turn right. The entrance to the museum will be on your right, almost immediately.

To Berry College: Stay on Highway 27 instead of turning onto Georgia Loop 1. In about half a mile, you will see the entrance to the college on the left. The second entrance, labeled "Main Entrance," is best.

As MIRACLES GO, THIS ONE MAY SEEM TAME. There was no bolt of lightning, no sudden revelation, no water changed to wine. This is a slower, more satisfying story of how one woman's faith enabled her to overcome opposition and skepticism. The school Martha Berry founded in 1902 with a gift of eighty-three acres now occupies 26,500 acres; it is said to be the largest college campus in the world.

No brief recap can convey the full Martha Berry story. But it can be richly experienced with a visit to the Martha Berry Museum, the Oak Hill Plantation next door, where she lived from her birth almost until her death, and a tour of the campus—preferably in that order.

A visit to the museum begins with a thirty-minute film on Berry's life. She was about twenty when three illiterate mountain boys knocked on the window of her "playhouse" on the plantation grounds. The boys were astonished when she told them there were stories in the Bible. She read to them, and the next week they were back, with their friends in tow.

Martha Berry's playhouse on this plantation, which is called Oak Hill, was the birthplace of the dream that grew into Berry College. The college is now said to have the largest campus in the world.

Soon Berry renovated an abandoned church to accommodate her growing Sunday school, and in 1902 she founded Berry College. Theodore Roosevelt came to visit. Henry Ford built a whole complex of buildings. The school, which began as a rich girl's effort to educate the mountain folk, has been ranked among the best in the country.

The museum is chock full of Martha Berry mementos. She knew every president from Teddy Roosevelt to FDR. The dress she wore when she was presented to the king and queen of England is on display. Here, too, are lesser-known artifacts, such as Henry Ford's jew's-harp and sleigh bells.

Martha Berry's older sister, Eugenia, married an Italian prince and moved to a castle not far from Rome, Italy. When she returned shortly before World War I, she brought with her ancient treasures, including a chest of drawers from the year 1100, said to have contained the relics of saints. These treasures fill a room of the museum.

A tour of Oak Hill, the plantation where Berry lived almost until her death in 1942, is included with the museum admission price. The airy elegance of the antebellum home and the sweeping grounds may prompt you to offer all the money you'll ever make for a chance to live there.

The home is bounded by spectacular gardens. If it's mid-April, call. The staff will tell you whether the thousands of azaleas are in bloom.

Tourists are welcome to drive through the sprawling campus. Skip the original entrance, the tree-lined "Gate of Opportunity." Drive instead a half mile down the road to the new main entrance. A few hundred yards down the entrance road stands a small brick guardhouse where you can get a map and have your questions answered.

Of particular interest on campus: Three beautiful chapels, all open to the public; Martha Berry's grave under a pecan tree outside the Mount Berry Chapel; the grave of Rony the Pony, who used to pull her to the renovated church where she first held Sunday school; the Ford Complex (where you will also find a handicraft store stocked with handwoven rugs, bathmats, placemats, scarves, camera straps, and what-have-you); and the Old Mill, which is powered by one of the largest overshot water wheels in the world.

Also of interest is the House o' Dreams atop Lavender Mountain. Built as a retreat for Martha Berry on the highest point in the county, it is open to the public. Call the museum ahead of time to get the key.

Be advised: Picnicking on campus is allowed only in a single designated picnic area.

MARTHA BERRY MUSEUM AND OAK HILL
189 Mount Berry Station
Mount Berry, GA 30149-0189
(706) 291-1883

HOURS: 10 A.M. to 5 P.M. Tuesday through Saturday; 1 P.M. to 5 P.M. Sunday.
ADMISSION: Adults $3; Children 6–12, $1.50; Children younger than 6, free.

HANDICAPPED ACCESS: The first floor of the museum, which is virtually everything, is accessible. The first floor of the plantation home is accessible, but the second floor is not.
FOOD: Groups of ten or more can order lunch in advance.
RESTROOMS: Yes.

BERRY COLLEGE CAMPUS
189 Mount Berry Station
Mount Berry, GA 30149-0189
(706) 291-1883

HOURS: Open to the public during daylight hours.
ADMISSION: Free.
HANDICAPPED ACCESS: Largely a driving tour.
FOOD: Snack bar (and bookstore) located in the Krannert Center; ask a guard at the front gate to direct you.
RESTROOMS: Yes.

Chieftains Museum
Rome
65 miles

Just after passing the Days Inn, turn right off 27 (Turner McCall Boulevard) toward the visitor center. At the stop sign, turn left. Follow this road to the bottom of the hill, where it ends at a duck pond. Turn right onto Riverside Parkway. Go 3 miles; the Chieftains Museum will be on your left.

THIS SMALL MUSEUM WAS THE HOME OF MAJOR Ridge, a prominent Cherokee leader who played an important role in the infamous Trail of Tears, the forced march of the Cherokee from Georgia to Oklahoma, on which four thousand people died.

Ridge was a prosperous fellow. He expanded this house from a log cabin, which had been built in 1794, into a Piedmont planter's house. He ran a ferry, owned thirty slaves, and presided over 288 acres.

But when gold was discovered on Cherokee land in Dahlonega (see the Dahlonega entry, page 107, for more on North America's first gold rush), the state of Georgia took the Cherokee land.

Ridge supported ceding land in the Southeast in exchange for a guarantee of permanent land in the West. About 16,000 ill-equipped Cherokee began the long march to Oklahoma; about one quarter of them died en route. Those who arrived were irate, and they killed Ridge and his family.

This two-story museum has artifacts from Ridge's career, as well as from the Coosa Indians, who preceded the Cherokee and were seen here by the Spanish explorer Hernando de Soto in 1540.

CHIEFTAINS MUSEUM
501 Riverside Parkway
P.O. Box 373
Rome, GA 30161
(706) 291-9494

HOURS: Tuesday through Friday, 10 A.M. to 4 P.M.; Sunday, 1 P.M. to 4 P.M.
ADMISSION: The requested donation is $3 for adults, $1.50 for children.
HANDICAPPED ACCESS: Downstairs only.
FOOD: No.
RESTROOMS: Yes.

Cave Spring

Cave Spring
81 miles

From Rome: Continue south on U.S. 411 for 16 miles until you reach Cave Spring.

THE TOWN DRAWS ITS NAME FROM AN IM-pressive limestone cave and the spring within. Each is reason enough to visit this town of fewer than one thousand residents; still another is the town's collection of artists and antique dealers.

The cave, located in Rolater Park at the center of town, is well lit and fun to explore. Stalactites hang from the ceiling, water oozes from the cave's limestone pores, and the 57-degree coolness offers a break from the heat of a summer day in Georgia.

The spring inside the cave produces three to four million gallons of water a day, supplying much of the surrounding area with drinking water and filling an adjacent 1.5-acre swimming pool, which also offers relief from summer heat. (You'll find the water a tad cooler than in the pool at your local motel.) People travel for miles to fill jugs with the water, which is also bottled and distributed commercially. It won't cure arthritis, so far as we know, but it tastes good.

More than forty antique and collectibles stores are located in the tiny town, many of them downtown. Two shops we recommend: Ironwood Fine Arts Studio Foundry, where Becky Davis creates bronze sculptures; and Kudzu Pottery Farm, which sells gorgeous dishes and other pottery items.

To reach the Kudzu Pottery Farm, take U.S. 411 and 52 west out of Cave Spring. Go 1 mile to the junction with Georgia 100 north (Fosters Mill Road). Turn right onto Highway 100. Go 1.3 miles. As the road turns to the left, look for a white barn with a red brick house and a Kudzu Pottery Farm sign on the right. Take the first unpaved driveway past the sign.

If you are coming from Rome, you will find the Ironwood studio shortly before you reach the town of Cave Spring. At the 7-mile marker on U.S. 411, turn left on Davis Road. At the top of the hill, after the road makes a 90-degree turn to the left, take the third driveway on the left. There are three houses there; the studio is in the blue house, which cannot be seen from the road.

If you plan to stay overnight in the area, try the Hearn Academy Inn, a bed and breakfast that shares Rolater Park with the cave and the swimming pool. Built in 1839, the five-room inn has wood floors, a sun-room where you can eat the continental breakfast, and a porch with rocking chairs for you to relax.

CITY OF CAVE SPRING
P.O. Box 365
Cave Spring, GA 30124
(706) 777-3382

ROLATER PARK
(706) 777-8439

HOURS: 11 A.M. to 5 P.M. daily during the summer; weekends
   only during the spring and fall; closed during the winter.
ADMISSION: Cave: $1; Pool: $2.
HANDICAPPED ACCESS: Park, yes; Cave, no.

THE HEARN ACADEMY INN
P.O. Box 715
Cave Spring, GA 30124
(706) 777-8865

IRONWOOD FINE ARTS STUDIO FOUNDRY
P.O. Box 130
Cave Spring, GA 30124
(706) 777-8772

HOURS: Usually open from 9 A.M. to 5 P.M., but call to be
   sure.

KUDZU POTTERY FARM
5093 Fosters Mill Road
Cave Spring, GA 30124
(706) 777-8789

HOURS: Tuesday through Saturday, 10 A.M. to 5 P.M.

Finster Art Studio

Summerville
80 miles

From Rome: Take Highway 27 north through Summerville. After passing the Smiles Convenience Store on the right, take the third available right turn onto Rena Street. Finster's Art Studio is at the end of Rena Street on the right.

IT'S A PRETTY SAFE BET YOU'VE NEVER SEEN anything quite like Howard Finster's art garden. Or like Howard Finster's Art Studio, for that matter.

The Reverend Mr. Finster began his prolific painting career in 1976 and soon found himself hailed as a folk art genius by national art critics. He paints and paints, covering wood cutouts, banners, posters, walls—nearly anything in his path. His art is in the Smithsonian. He's done album covers for REM and Talking Heads. His art studio is chock full of his works. Prices range from $35 to $3,500.

The four acres around the studio—"Paradise Garden," Finster calls it—border on bizarre. Sculptures made of rusted bicycle parts, hubcaps, and other scraps loom over walkways embedded with glass, tile, beads, and seashells. Even old automobiles that seem to have stood in Finster's path while he was in the grip of inspiration are covered with painted figures, biblical verses, or messages.

Finster paints six days a week while other family members mind the studio. On the seventh day he runs the studio and greets the public, so Sunday is the day to go if you want to meet the artist.

FINSTER ART STUDIO
Howard Finster
Route 2, Box 106-A
Summerville, GA 30747
(706) 857-2926

HOURS: 10 A.M. to 6 P.M., seven days a week.
ADMISSION: Free.
HANDICAPPED ACCESS: No.
FOOD: No.
RESTROOMS: Yes.

Dalton: Carpet Capital of the World

Dalton
88 miles

From Atlanta: Take Interstate 75 north to exit 135. Turn left, to cross to the other side of the interstate, and you will find yourself in the middle of carpet outlet heaven.

BEFORE WORLD WAR II, CARPET WAS A LUXURY only the wealthy could afford. But the invention of the tufting machine and the manufacture of inexpensive manmade fibers changed that—and put Dalton on the map. Fully 65 percent of the carpet in the world is manufactured in this area. It is an $8 billion-per-year industry, employing 40,000 people.

This mammoth industry sprang from the humble chore of making bedspreads in the home. The tufting machine was invented, partly in response to wage and hour laws, to put chenille patterns on the bedspreads. Modern tufting machines use hundreds of needles to insert fibers into a backing material and make carpets twenty-five times faster than looms. Manmade fibers are cheaper than wool. Now, 95 percent of carpet is tufted; 98 percent is made with artificial fibers.

There are more than 100 carpet outlets in the Dalton area. According to industry spokespeople, you can buy your carpet here, have it shipped home to Detroit or California or wherever, and still spend less than had you shopped locally. Where do you think your local store buys the carpet it sells, anyway?

How to choose from among 100 outlets? One way is to pick up a list of those that are members of the Dalton Carpet & Rug Outlet Council. The flier can be obtained by calling, writing, or visiting the Northwest Georgia Trade & Convention Center. The phone number is 1-800-824-7469. The address is P.O. Box 2046, Dalton, GA 30722. To pick up the flier (and other brochures) go one more exit. Get off Interstate 75 at Exit 136. Go left, over the highway. Stay on that road, up the hill. The trade center will be on your left.

New Echota Historic Site

Calhoun
75 miles

From Atlanta: Take Interstate 75 north to Calhoun, Exit 131. Take Highway 225 east about one-half mile.

A SERENE SADNESS ENGULFS THE PLACE WHERE a nation's capital was born and a tragedy began. For some, it marks the high point of the Cherokee Nation, a sovereign country within the newly minted United States. For others, the site is a place of shame, a reminder of the abuse and mistreatment of the American Indian.

The Cherokee, following the philosophy of "if-you-can't-beat-'em-join-'em," patterned their nation after the American government. They had a judicial system that included a supreme court, and a representative form of government with its house and senate. They were the first Native Americans to devise their own alphabet, which led in 1828 to the establishment of a newspaper, the *Cherokee Phoenix.*

But the discovery of gold on Cherokee land in 1828 was the beginning of the end of the Cherokee attempt to protect their sovereignty by imitating the white man. The gold rush into Indian territory ultimately resulted in the confiscation of Cherokee land by the state of Georgia, which then auctioned it off to white prospectors and farmers.

Still playing by the rules, the Cherokee appealed the land seizure through the American court system, ultimately reaching the U.S. Supreme Court, which sided with the Cherokee.

Tough, responded President Andrew Jackson, who refused to follow the Supreme Court decision with a terse rebuttal of Chief Justice John Marshall's opinion that the land must be returned to the Indians: "John Marshall has made his decision. Now let him enforce it."

In this early test of the nation's system of checks and balances, the system failed. Overruling the Supreme Court, Jackson ordered the military roundup of Cherokee in Georgia and North Carolina.

They left New Echota in 1838 on the 800-mile Trail of Tears march to Oklahoma in which four thousand Indians died.

As the capital of a short-lived democracy, New Echota was too new to be much of a town. There were only seventy-five residents in the town at its peak. But in its piece-by-piece re-creation of the settlement, the state-owned historic site gives visitors a sense of what the place was like. There's the small, one-room newspaper office where the *Phoenix* was printed, and the white two-story building where the Cherokee Supreme Court sat. A Cherokee-style homestead, with its vegetable garden and unpainted buildings, has been re-created, as well as an old-style tavern and inn.

Down a gravel trail remains the only original building left from the glory days of New Echota. The Worcester house, the home of a white missionary who suffered for his support of the Cherokees, served as a post office, school, and boarding house before being confiscated by the state of Georgia.

The historic site welcome center gives an overview of the events leading to New Echota's founding and its demise with exhibits and a fifteen-minute film.

Soaked in tragedy and betrayal, New Echota nonetheless is a tranquil place, a quiet and picturesque reminder of a failed attempt to get along peacefully.

NEW ECHOTA HISTORIC SITE
1211 Chatsworth Highway
Calhoun, GA 30701
(706) 629-8151

ADMISSION: Adults, $1.50; Children 6–18, seventy-five cents; Children 5 and younger, free.
HOURS: Tuesday through Saturday, 9 A.M. to 5 P.M.; Sunday, 2 P.M. to 5:30 P.M.
HANDICAPPED ACCESS: One step, but no ramps to museum. Paths unpaved.
FOOD: No.
RESTROOMS: Yes.

Chief Vann House

Chatsworth
90 miles

From Atlanta: Take Interstate 75 north to Calhoun, Exit 131. Take Highway 225 north about 18 miles.

IT SITS MAJESTICALLY ON THE TOP OF A HILL, A big, two-story brick mansion built in 1804 by an Indian chief. A hard-drinking but prosperous farmer and merchant, Chief James Vann was a rich and mercurial man who once had his favorite slave whipped nearly to death and then burned at the stake for theft.

The house, huge from the outside, is mostly four big rooms: a dining room, living room, master bedroom, and guest bedroom. The numerous Vann children occupied two dormitory-like bedrooms in the attic. In the basement is a combination wine cellar and dungeon.

The first floor is divided into two rooms, separated by a wide hallway and an unusual cantilevered staircase whose support-less construction still mystifies architects. The downstairs rooms have high ceilings and are decorated in symbolic Cherokee colors of green (grass and trees), yellow (harvest fields), blue (sky), and red (soil). They were used as Vann's dining and living rooms. The rooms are nearly as colorful as the stories that accompany the house and its occupants.

Shot to death in a tavern, Chief Vann left his house and most of his property to his youngest son, Joseph, whose own subsequent success earned him the nickname "Rich Joe."

Rich Joe lost the house and property in 1830 when he hired a white man to oversee his plantation, thus violating a Georgia law that made it illegal for a white person to work for an Indian. Joseph Vann appealed the seizure of his property and eventually won a $19,605 settlement from the U.S. government. He used the money to build a replica of the Vann house in Oklahoma; it was destroyed during the Civil War.

Rich Joe, a gambler who owned racehorses, met an untimely death in 1844 when a steamboat he owned blew up on the Ohio River in a race against another steamboat. Fearful of losing a bet on the race, Vann had ordered a slave to stoke the furnace with the last available fuel: a side of beef. After failing to convince Vann that this was not a good idea, the slave did as instructed and then jumped overboard before the grease in the meat caused the boiler to explode. Vann, and his favorite racehorse, Lucy Walker, died in the explosion; the slave lived.

After Rich Joe's eviction, the Vann mansion became the subject of a dispute that led to a hallway shootout between the two conflicting owners. The winner succeeded in smoking out his rival from an upstairs bedroom by placing a burning log on the stairs, which still bear the burn marks.

By 1952, the first brick house built in the Cherokee Nation had become just another vacant and vandalized building. Purchased by a local historical society and donated to the Georgia Historical Commission, the home was restored and opened to the public in 1958.

Sealed in glass cases inside the downstairs hallway are Vann family artifacts recovered during the mansion's restoration. Included in the display are shattered fragments of the family china, sad remnants of wasted wealth and misspent lives.

CHIEF VANN HOUSE
Route 7, Box 7655
Chatsworth, GA 30705
(706) 695-2598

HOURS: Tuesday through Saturday, 9 A.M. to 5 P.M.; Sunday, 2 P.M. to 5:30 P.M.
ADMISSION: Adults, $1.50; Children 6–18, seventy-five cents; Children 5 and younger, free.
HANDICAPPED ACCESS: No.
FOOD: No.
RESTROOMS: Yes.

Cloudland Canyon
State Park

Rising Fawn
109 miles

From Atlanta: Take Interstate 75 north to Exit 133; take Highway 136 east to Highway 27; take Highway 27 north to Highway 136; take Highway 136 to Cloudland Canyon State Park.

GEORGIA IS A STATE FILLED WITH BEAUTIFUL parks and recreation areas, but the most breathtaking of them all almost belongs to Tennessee. Tucked into the northwest corner of the state, just twenty-five miles south of Chattanooga, the 2,120-acre park straddles Sitton Gulch Creek—a pretty, small river at the bottom of a pretty, deep canyon.

From the edge of the canyon cliffs, the river is invisible, hidden beneath the cloak of trees that in autumn looks like a paint-splattered shroud of orange, red, yellow, and green.

The park has twelve miles of trails, including a five-mile loop along the rim of the canyon. Hikers can walk around the edge of the canyon, descend one thousand feet from the peak of the park to the floor of the river, and climb back up the side of the canyon to the opposite rim.

At the bottom of the canyon, the creek courses over two waterfalls, one that tumbles one hundred feet into a picturesque pool below. It's the kind of place that makes you feel like you're living inside a television commercial.

The park prohibits swimming in the waterfall pool, but assuages the urge to take a dip by providing a chlorinated swimming pool on the park grounds that is open during the summer. Pool admission is $1.25 per person. The park has tennis courts, too. The courts are free.

The park has seventy-five tent and trailer campsites, thirty primitive campsites, and sixteen fully equipped two- and three-bedroom cabins that require reservations eleven months in advance if you want to occupy one during the leaf-turning season.

Park gates are locked at 10 P.M. and don't open again until 7 A.M., so get there early and don't stay out too late. Although there are a couple of country stores nearby, the closest supermarket is in Trenton, eight miles away.

Other state parks in Georgia might have higher waterfalls and taller mountains, but for pure scenic splendor, none can match Cloudland Canyon.

CLOUDLAND CANYON STATE PARK
Route 2, Box 150
Rising Fawn, GA 30738
(706) 657-4050

HOURS: Daily, 7 A.M. to 10 P.M.; park office hours, 8 A.M. to 9 P.M.
ADMISSION: $2 per car for park pass; $10 per night for tent and trailer campsites; $50 to $70 per night for cabins.
HANDICAPPED ACCESS: Handicapped camping facilities available.
FOOD: Vending machines only.
RESTROOMS: Yes, including showers.

Chickamauga and Chattanooga National Military Park

Fort Oglethorpe
115 miles

From Atlanta: Take Interstate 75 north to Exit 141; take State Road 2 west to Fort Ogelthorpe; take Highway 27 1 mile south to the military park.

THERE IS STILL ENOUGH OF THE BATTLEFIELD left—5,500 acres—for the twentieth century to recede behind the trees. There aren't any television antennas, rooftops, or high-rises to ruin the illusion of what it must have been like 130 years ago before two armies turned the fields and woods into one of the bloodiest battlegrounds of the Civil War.

"Most of the time you are not insulted by the twentieth century too much. It's not like some battlefields around Atlanta where almost nothing is left at all," said Jim Ogden, park historian. "Here you can still get a real sense of what occurred. You can picture in your mind the thousands of troops moving here or there."

For two days in September 1863, 124,000 men in uniforms of gray and blue fought for control of this pivotal patch of real estate that borders the slender Chickamauga Creek.

Four thousand of the men died; 24,000 were wounded. Monuments erected by the states—North and South—that lost men in the battle outline the battlefield positions of the opposing forces. Sometimes enemies were separated by little more than the width of the two-lane road.

When the gunsmoke cleared, the Confederates claimed victory. But it was such a costly battle they were unable to pursue the fleeing Union forces, who retreated long enough to regroup, gain reinforcements, and capture strategic Lookout Mountain and Chattanooga's railroad hub. The Union defeat that led to a victory opened the gates to the Deep South for Gen. William T. Sherman and started his march toward Atlanta and the sea.

A twenty-six-minute multimedia presentation at the National Park Service Visitor Center tells the story of the Battle of Chickamauga—its tactical blunders and its battlefield heroics—through the eyes of Union and Confederate soldiers brought back together for an 1889 reunion. The battlefield park was created a year later. "The Civil War is the turning point in American history, and by understanding this campaign we can understand how the Civil War was fought and won," Ogden said.

The battleground is studded with 1,400 monuments, markers, and plaques, and 250 cannon. The best way to view the battlefield is via the seven-mile auto tour. But don't just drive through. Get out of the car, read the markers, and imagine a place of pastoral tranquility—just before all hell broke loose.

CHICKAMAUGA AND CHATTANOOGA NATIONAL
   MILITARY PARK
P.O. Box 2128
Fort Ogelthorpe, GA 30742
(706) 866-9241

HOURS: 8 A.M. to 4:45 P.M. daily.
ADMISSION: Free. Multimedia program, Adults, $2.25;
   Seniors, $1; Children younger than 16, $1.
HANDICAPPED ACCESS: Yes.
FOOD: No.
RESTROOMS: Yes.

CHAPTER FIVE

THE COAST

COASTAL GEORGIA IS ABOUT AS FAR AWAY from Atlanta as you can get, both in distance and in ambiance. No office towers dwarf the treetops. No traffic jams. Some places are even inaccessible by car. No night life, except the type that squeaks, chirps, and croaks in the darkness.

The Georgia coast is the land of the three-day weekend and week-long vacation. It's not a place you rush to or rush through. It takes its time, approaches things leisurely. And you should, too.

The thirteen barrier islands along Georgia's 115-mile coast set their clocks to the moods of the moon, which pulls and tugs at the tides. This is the region of sunsets, sea breezes, and salt marshes.

Each island has something different to offer, each its own personality. From the low-rent casualness of Tybee Island to the hoity-toity exclusivity of Sea Island, coastal Georgia spans the spectrum of beach life.

Rich industrialists once treated coastal Georgia as their private kingdom, buying up whole islands and surrounding themselves, moat-style, with water like medieval kings. In the glory years of the Golden Isles, John D. Rockefeller handed dimes to schoolchildren at the train depot in Darien.

When the wealthy retreated, they left behind souvenirs of their affluence: golf courses, tennis courts, horse stables, and castle-like island homes. In 1947, the state of Georgia bought Jekyll Island for $675,000—about the price of one of the mansion-like cottages left behind—in one of the best real estate deals since the Indians handed over Manhattan.

The heirs to the legacy of the Golden Isles are the tourists who now pay to take a peek at what the wealthy no longer want.

While Jekyll Island contains the residue of the rich, Sapelo Island is still home to the descendants of slaves who maintain their African culture in the community of Hog Hammock. The rest of the island, including the old sugar cane and cotton fields, has been preserved as a wildlife sanctuary.

For those who like some civilization mixed in with their relaxation, there is William T. Sherman's Christmas present to Abraham Lincoln: Savannah. A little bit like New Orleans without the decadence, Savannah was once described as a "pretty lady with a dirty face." Savannah has gussied itself up since then: The restoration of its old houses has created the largest historic residential district in the country.

But if you're looking to get away from electricity altogether, coastal Georgia fits that bill, too. The Okefenokee Swamp—headwaters of the Suwannee and home to Pogo—is a leftover from the beginning of time, a dark and wondrous place of moss-draped cypress, snakes, alligators, and mosquitoes. Having failed to tame and drain the swamp, mankind is restricted to nesting around its edges and taking camping and canoeing excursions into its primordial heart.

Savannah

Savannah
252 miles

From Atlanta: Take Interstate 75 south to Macon; from Macon, take Interstate 16 east to Savannah.

THIS CITY HAS BEEN AROUND A LONG TIME, longer in fact than any other city in Georgia. Savannah is a city to savor.

Savannah was geometrically laid out on a grid pattern of twenty-four residential squares by James Oglethorpe in 1733. The city has retained much of its original colonial charm through the preservation of its squares, restoration of its eighteenth- and nineteenth-century homes, and perpetual cultivation of its many gardens.

With twenty-three historic inns and guest houses—everything from bed-and-breakfast inns to carriage houses to European-style hotels—Savannah calls itself "the Inn City." But then, it also calls itself "the Garden City," "the Walking City," "the Dining City," and "the Festival City."

The best place to get your first taste of this old port-city-of-many-names is the Savannah Visitor Center, housed in the Central Station train depot built in 1861. The visitor center has a sixteen-minute slide show on the city's history. The show costs $1 for adults, fifty cents for children six to twelve, and is free for those under six.

The train depot also contains the Savannah Historical Museum, which displays artifacts, memorabilia, and exhibits that trace the city's history from its American Indian occupation through the 1930s.

The depot is the departure point for historic tours of the city. The tours range from one to two-and-a-half hours. Tours are available by bus, trolley, carriage, bicycle, and on foot. Although most of the tours cover the same historic streets and buildings, one tour specializes in the black heritage of the city, and another offers a four-hour salt marsh excursion to Tybee Island and back.

The Black Heritage Trail Tour includes a stop at the 1896 King-Tisdell Cottage, which serves as both the heritage tour's headquarters and a museum of black history along the Georgia coast. Although Georgia was the only one of the thirteen original colonies initially to prohibit slavery, Savannah was a port in the slave trade as early as 1749. The docks where the slave ships arrived are part of the black heritage tour, as is the spot where William T. Sherman made his famous speech promising that after the Civil War every former slave would receive "forty acres and a mule."

The city's various tours offer a quick overview of what Savannah has to offer: its historic homes, monument-studded series of residential squares and parks, museums, restored waterfront district, city market, restaurants, and saloons. The city's 2.5-square-mile historic district contains 1,100 historic buildings and 2,300 structures designated as historically significant.

After the tour, go back to the places of interest you passed by. A walk down Bull Street, the oldest street in Georgia, is a stroll down the backbone of Savannah's historic district. The street passes many of the city's most picturesque squares, monuments, shops, and homes.

Many of the tours include admission to one or two house museums. One of the most popular residences is the Juliette Gordon Low House, home of the founder of the Girl Scouts.

Another favorite stop is the Davenport House, where Cornelia Davenport Jackson, recovering from childbirth, died after eating a tainted meal prepared by a well-wishing neighbor. Definitely a case of the cure being worse than the disease.

Savannah is filled with such stories. Tour guides still talk about the scandalous rumors that swept through the city when the wife of Nathanael Greene, second in command to George Washington, took a liking to a clever young man named Eli Whitney, who later invented the cotton gin. There are also stories about the disreputable Pirate's Tavern, an old hangout for the Blackbeard set in 1753,

Stately eighteenth- and nineteenth-century houses are sprinkled throughout Savannah's 2.5-square-mile historic district that boasts 1,100 historic buildings.

and a paranormal house at 507 East St. Julian Street, where ghosts are thought to play.

"Everybody takes it very seriously," said tour guide Loretta Lominack, who lives nearby. "And nobody tricks or treats there on Halloween."

The most famous of all Savannah stories, however, is the saga of the "waving girl," who was—depending on which version you believe—either very lovesick or very bored. For fifty years, Florence Martus waved to every incoming and departing ship, with a flag during the day and a lantern at night. The sister of a lighthouse tender on an isolated island, Martus was rumored to be awaiting the return of a sailor she loved, hoping that each ship that came into Savannah was bringing him back. According to Martus herself, she started waving to ships out of boredom and it just became a habit that evolved into a tradition. When her brother retired from the lighthouse, Martus stopped waving. She died, unmarried, in 1943.

A statue of the waving girl, designed by the artist who created the Iwo Jima monument in Washington, DC, faces the Savannah River in the city's riverfront park.

Sitting nearly dead-center in the historic district is the Colonial Park Cemetery, where many prominent Savannah residents, including one or two who signed the Declaration of Independence, are buried. Although Union general William T. Sherman spared Savannah from destruction, his men were a bit hard on the cemetery where they pastured their mules. Not only did the mules knock over and destroy numerous gravestones, but mischievous soldiers also switched tombstones on some graves.

Nearly a dozen churches and temples in Savannah date back to 1800, including the First American Baptist Church, where blacks being smuggled north through the Underground Railroad were hidden beneath floorboards spiked with breathing holes for ventilation. The city has a sizable Jewish population, which built the Temple Mickve Israel in 1878. Jews have been accepted in Savannah since its inception, but Catholics were banned from the city until shortly before the Revolutionary War because of British fears that they would conspire with the Spanish colonies in Florida and the French colonies in Canada.

The tours pass by the City Market, a collection of gift shops, galleries, and restaurants situated in a restored warehouse district. Most shops close by 6 P.M., but the market doesn't go to bed until the jazz and blues clubs close.

The tours usually end on the riverfront, where the ground floors of the city's old three-story cotton warehouses abut cobblestone streets made from the ballast of the first ships to arrive from England. The street is lined with seventy-five restaurants, pubs, and gift shops. It is also home to the four-story Ships of the Sea Museum, one of the best maritime museums in the nation.

During the summers, a riverfront tavern conducts a Savannah tradition: whacking golf balls into the Savannah River. Every Friday, amateur golfers pay to pelt the river with golf balls in the long-shot chance of winning a new car. It's not the same as watching the sun set on Mallory Dock in Key West, but in a town built around attracting tourists, it does draw a crowd.

Savannah Visitor Center
303 Martin Luther King, Jr., Blvd.
Savannah, GA 31401
(912) 944-0456

Savannah History Museum
(912) 238-1779

Hours: Monday through Friday, 8:30 A.M. to 5 P.M.; Saturday
  and Sunday, 9 A.M. to 5 P.M.
Admission: Adults, $3; Seniors and Military, $2.50; Children
  6–12, $1.75; Children 5 and younger, free.
Handicapped Access: Yes.
Food: Snack bar.
Restrooms: Yes.

Ships of the Sea Museum
503 East River Street
Savannah, GA 31401
(912) 232-1511

Hours: Daily, 10 A.M. to 5 P.M.
Admission: Adults, $3; Children 7–12, $1.50; Children 6
  and younger, free.
Handicapped Access: Top and bottom floor entrances only.
Food: No.
Restrooms: Yes.

Juliette Gordon Low House
142 Bull Street
Savannah, GA 31401
(912) 233-4501

Hours: Monday through Saturday, 10 A.M. to 4 P.M.; Sunday,
  12:30 P.M. to 4:30 P.M. Closed Wednesday.
Admission: Adults, $5; Children 6–18, $4; Children 5 and
  younger, free; Girl Scouts, $1 off; Seniors, $4.50.
Handicapped Access: First floor only.
Restrooms: Yes.

Fort Pulaski National Monument

Savannah
64 miles

From Savannah: Take Highway 80 east 12 miles.

IT TOOK EIGHTEEN YEARS TO BUILD A FORT AS "strong as the Rocky Mountains" and only thirty hours of bombardment to prove its vincibility. An experimental cannon ripped holes in the brick walls of Fort Pulaski with bullet-shaped projectiles fired by Union soldiers a mile away.

Fort Pulaski's military claim to fame was that it proved, to the dismay of 385 Confederate soldiers inside, that the era of masonry forts was over.

But its preservation as a national monument since 1924 gives an estimated 400,000 visitors a year the chance to see a fort with an almost artistic appeal. A failure as a fort, the structure succeeds as art.

"It was obviously designed for war, but the people building the fort also took the extra step to make it architecturally pleasing," said park superintendent John Breen. "It has amazing symmetry."

The fort is as angular as the twenty-five million bricks that make up its walls, and as curved as the semi-circular grooves along which its cannon pivoted. Along one side, the first-floor pillars are square brick columns; on other sides they are topped with graceful arches. Some stairways leading to the second level are rectangular, others are spiral.

Within its walls, the fort tells the story of the soldiers who occupied it, first as its defenders and then as its prisoners. There are the hard, wood-plank bunk beds of the enlisted men and the commander's quarters decorated by his wife with furniture confiscated from village homes. There are the storerooms converted by Union troops into prison cells for their Confederate captives, and the cool, dark storerooms where the powder and cannonballs were kept. There are the long mess tables with plates, bowls, and cups stacked neatly, waiting for the next meal.

A giant oak anchors a corner of the grassy field in the center of the fort, casting cool shade on the benches for visitors below.

The fort, built on a marshy rise called Cockspur Island, over-looks 5,600 acres of the national park, which includes picnic areas, nature trails, and fishing piers.

On the way to and from Fort Pulaski, you'll pass another historic Savannah fortification: Old Fort Jackson. The oldest fort in Georgia, Old Fort Jackson traces its foundation back to 1775, when it was an earthen battery unit. A brick fort was built in 1808 and enlarged between 1845 and 1860. During the Civil War, the fort served as headquarters for the Confederate defense of the river.

Today, the fort guards only a picturesque view of the Savannah River.

FORT PULASKI NATIONAL MONUMENT
P.O. Box 30757
Savannah, GA 31410-0757
(912) 786-5787

HOURS: Daily, 8:30 P.M. to 5:30 P.M.
ADMISSION: $2 per person, $4 per family; Seniors, free with Golden Age passport; Handicapped, free with Golden Access passport; Children 16 and younger, free.
HANDICAPPED ACCESS: Visitor center and first floor of fort; top floor of fort inaccessible to wheelchairs.
FOOD: No, but picnic facilities available.
RESTROOMS: Yes.

OLD FORT JACKSON
Old Fort Jackson
1 Fort Jackson Road
Savannah, GA 31414
(912) 232-3945

HOURS: Daily, 9 A.M. to 5 P.M.
ADMISSION: Adults, $2.50; Students, Military, and Seniors, $2; Children 5 and younger, free.
HANDICAPPED ACCESS: Yes.
FOOD: No.
RESTROOMS: Yes.

Tybee Island

Tybee Island
268 miles

From Savannah: Take Highway 80 east until you hit the Atlantic Ocean.

THE 178 STEPS WIND IN A RED SPIRAL STAIR-case inside the tube of whitewashed brick that forms the oldest and tallest lighthouse in Georgia. Along the way up the 154-foot tower, window alcoves provide a view of the Atlantic Ocean to the east and the cluster of lighthouse tender buildings below.

Heir to the original lighthouse commissioned by Savannah founder James Ogelthorpe in 1739, the current Tybee Lighthouse was built in two phases: the first sixty feet in 1773 and the next ninety-four feet in 1867. Burning a one-thousand-watt bulb magnified through the prisms of a ten-foot Fresnel lens, the lighthouse beacon can be seen by ships as far as eighteen miles off shore.

Before the Civil War, federal troops on Tybee Island were punished for drunkenness by being loaded down with a weighted knapsack and ordered to march around the base of the lighthouse. Before Union troops re-took the island, Confederates retreating to Fort Pulaski blew up the top half of the lighthouse.

The lighthouse's last keeper, George Jackson, died in 1948. The fully automated lighthouse is owned and operated by the U.S. Coast Guard.

A short distance from the lighthouse are the last remaining coastal gun batteries built in the 1890s as part of Fort Screven, which closed in 1945. Battery Brumby, built between 1897 and 1898, was the first and largest of seven gun batteries at Fort Screven, all designed to protect the mouth of the Savannah River from attack. The battery boasted eight guns capable of hitting a ship ten miles at sea. The guns, however, were never used. Shipped to

France during World War I, they were never returned and the battery was used as storage until the fort closed.

Next to Battery Brumby is the Garland Battery, which now houses the Tybee Museum. Seven rooms inside the thick concrete walls of the battery have been turned into displays depicting the history of Tybee Island from its days as an Indian hunting ground and Blackbeard's treasure burial ground to the island's heyday as a resort in the 1920s and 1930s. The museum defines itself as a "community's attic" and proves it by including one local resident's doll collection and another's collection of guns and weapons.

TYBEE LIGHTHOUSE AND TYBEE MUSEUM
P.O. Box 366
Tybee Island, GA 31328
(912) 786-5801

HOURS: April 1 to Sept. 30, daily, 10 A.M. to 6 P.M.; Oct. 1 to March 31, Monday through Friday, noon to 4 P.M.; Saturday and Sunday, 10 A.M. to 4 P.M. Closed Tuesday.

ADMISSION: Adults, $2.50; Seniors 62 and older, $1.50; Children 6–12, seventy-five cents.

HANDICAPPED ACCESS: No.

FOOD: No. Picnic tables are situated at the lighthouse and access to the beach is behind the museum.

RESTROOMS: Yes.

Sapelo Island National Estuarine Sanctuary Tours

Darien
328 miles

From Atlanta: Take Interstate 75 south to Interstate 16. Take Interstate 16 east to Interstate 95. Take Interstate 95 south to Exit 10. Take Highway 17 south to the Darien Welcome Center at the intersection of Fort King George Drive.

SAPELO ISLAND ONCE BELONGED TO THE wealthy. A cotton plantation owner, Thomas Spaulding, was the first to buy it in 1802. His heirs sold the island to Hudson Motor Car manufacturer Howard Coffin, who sold it to tobacco king R.J. Reynolds, who built a mansion on the island.

Reynolds' mansion is still there, but the rich people are all gone. The only residents of the island are seventy-five descendants of Spaulding's four hundred slaves, who live in a community called Hog Hammock. Isolated from the rest of the world, Hog Hammock residents have retained much of their African heritage, including the painting of their houses brilliant colors to ward off evil spirits.

Except for Hog Hammock, the island now belongs to the state of Georgia, which has preserved Sapelo as one of the last un-developed barrier islands on the Georgia coast.

"There is no place on earth like it," said Mary Jo Goltz, executive director of the McIntosh Chamber of Commerce. "We hope to keep it that way."

After a thirty-minute ferry ride to the island, visitors find a place filled with wildlife instead of people. There are turkeys, deer, alligators, egrets, and eagles that have been released on the island as part of an eagle restoration program. The wildlife resides in the salt marshes, cotton and sugar cane fields, and pastures left behind by human residents.

The University of Georgia operates a marine institute started by R.J. Reynolds, who was interested in studying the marshes and their estuaries. The research continues today through the institute, which includes a small museum displaying the island's plant and animal life.

During the four-hour tours, visitors are taken through Hog Hammock, past Behaviour Cemetery (a slave burial ground still used by Hog Hammock residents), and around Spaulding's cotton, rice, and sugar cane fields, and shown the only beach in McIntosh County. Visitors are taken past the Reynolds' mansion and into the Marine Institute.

Longer tours, conducted once a month from March to October, take visitors to the north end of the island to view the ruins of a French plantation.

The tours are limited to 45 people, so reservations are required. And bring your own mosquito repellent.

SAPELO ISLAND NATIONAL ESTUARINE
   SANCTUARY TOURS
Darien Welcome Center
P.O. Box 734
Darien, GA 31305
(912) 437-6684

HOURS: Regular tours, Wednesday and Friday, 8:30 A.M. to 12:30 P.M., and Saturday, 9 A.M. to 1 P.M. Extended tours, March through October, last Tuesday of every month, 8:30 A.M. to 2:30 P.M.
ADMISSION: $5.50 per person: Children younger than 6, free.
HANDICAPPED ACCESS: No.
FOOD: Bring your own lunch for extended day tours.
RESTROOMS: Yes.

Jekyll Island and the Golden Isles

Jekyll Island
310 miles

From Atlanta: Take Interstate 75 south to Macon; take Interstate 16 east to Interstate 95 south; take Exit 6 to Jekyll Island.

JEKYLL ISLAND IS THE GOLDEST OF THE GOLDEN Isles, a place once so exclusively rich that even Winston Churchill and President William McKinley were denied membership.

The other islands have their assets:

Manhattan-size St. Simon's Island to the north is larger and has more golf courses, hotels, and restaurants. It also has Fort Frederica, built in 1736 by Savannah's founder, James Ogelthorpe; the 1872 St. Simon's Island Lighthouse; and Christ Church, an 1886 wooden Gothic church that still holds Episcopal church services.

Accessible only by boat, Little St. Simon's Island is less developed, offering overnight guests rustic cabins instead of name-brand hotels.

Sea Island is one of the most exclusive islands on the Georgia coast, occupied primarily by the five-star Cloister resort, where George and Barbara Bush spent their honeymoon in 1945. The nearby town of Brunswick has its historic district of restored Victorian homes and, of course, its famous concoction of chicken, pork, and vegetables called Brunswick stew.

But of them all, Jekyll Island is the jewel in the crown of Georgia's Golden Isles.

Sleep where millionaire robber barons once conspired at the Queen Anne-style Jekyll Island Clubhouse, built in 1887 and restored by the state of Georgia in 1986.

First thing: Ditch the car. Twenty miles of bike paths ring the perimeter of the island, which was once off limits to anyone but the richest robber barons.

These days, Jekyll Island is open to anyone who can afford the $2 parking fee. But a century ago, Jekyll Island belonged to the richest men in America. Pulitzer, Rockefeller, Morgan, Gould, and McCormick created the millionaires-only Jekyll Island Club and turned the island into a playground for themselves and their families. In 1904, it was described as "the richest, the most exclusive, the most inaccessible club in the world."

The centerpiece of their private retreat was the Queen Anne-style clubhouse, designed by Chicago architect Charles A. Alexander. Completed in 1887, the clubhouse had sixty guest rooms, wraparound porches, a circular tower, and was situated within a quarter mile of all fifty lots set aside for the millionaires to build their mansion-size "cottages."

The clubhouse has undergone a $20 million, state-funded restoration and rents its rooms these days to ordinary people for as little as $69—and as much as $229—a night.

William Rockefeller's 1892 Edwardian-style cottage mansion sits beside the Mistletoe Cottage, owned by railroad magnate Henry Kirk Porter, which is next door to the Goodyear Cottage, which belonged to the rubber baron. Several of the cottages are open for public tours, some are still private residences, and others are viewed from the tram tours that leave the Museum Orientation Center, which originally served as the club members' stables.

The museum offers a pictorial history of the 33-structure, 240-acre historic district and its ongoing renovation by the state of Georgia—the largest restoration project in the Southeast. A fifteen-minute film for those taking the tram tour provides a glimpse into the lives of the rich and famous of long ago. Ninety-minute tram tours leave the museum from 10 A.M. to 3 P.M.

The reign of the wealthy lasted from 1886 to 1942. The rich residents were at the peak of their influence in the days before World War I. On Jan. 25, 1915, the first transcontinental telephone call was made from Jekyll Island by the president of AT&T to Alexander Graham Bell in New York, Bell's assistant Thomas A. Watson in San Francisco, and President Woodrow Wilson in Washington, DC.

The advent of World War II ended the golden era, and in 1947 the luxurious clubhouse was closed. The state of Georgia took over operation of the hotel and restored it in 1986.

The historic district occupies only a portion of the island which, as a whole, offers a something-for-everyone resort. There are long, flat beaches, a summers-only eleven-acre water park, two miniature golf courses, four full-size golf courses totalling sixty-three holes, indoor and outdoor tennis courts, deep-sea fishing, hiking trails, restaurants, and shops.

The ten hotels on the island have rooms renting from $54 and up. Or you can rent a house—they call them "cottages," too—for $200 to $1,600 a week depending on the time of year and the number of bedrooms.

Campsites are available at the Jekyll Island Campground for $10 a night for tents, $13 a night for campers, and $15 a night for full-hookup RVs.

And if you forget to bring a bike, they rent those, too ($4.25 per hour, $10.25 per day).

MUSEUM ORIENTATION CENTER
375 Riverview Drive
Jekyll Island, GA 31527
(912) 635-4036

HOURS: Daily, 9:30 A.M. to 4 P.M.

ADMISSION: $2 per car parking fee to get on the island. Tram tours: Adults, $7; Children 6–18, $5; Children 5 and younger, free. Tour price includes fifteen-minute film.

HANDICAPPED ACCESS: For assistance contact the museum office at (912) 635-2119.

FOOD: Several restaurants on the island.

RESTROOMS: Yes.

Okefenokee National Wildlife Refuge

Waycross
238 miles

To the Okefenokee Swamp Park from Atlanta: Take Interstate 75 south to Tifton; take Highway 82 east to Waycross; take Highway 1 south 8 miles to State Road 177; turn right.

To the Laura S. Walker State Park from Atlanta: Take Interstate 75 south to Tifton; take highway 82 east to State Road 177; turn right.

To the Suwannee Canal Recreation Area from Atlanta: Take Interstate 75 south to Tifton; take Highway 82 east to Waycross; take Highway 1 south to Folkston; take State Road 121 south.

To the Stephen C. Foster State Park from Atlanta: Take Interstate 75 south from Atlanta to Exit 5 at Valdosta; take State Road 94 east to Fargo; take State Road 177 north.

THE OKEFENOKEE NATIONAL WILDLIFE REFUGE is one of the most foreboding—and beautiful—places in Georgia. Largely inaccessible without tour guides, the swamp covers 412,000 acres and engulfs about a third of Ware County. The swamp is the origination of two major estuaries, the St. Mary's and Suwannee rivers.

The refuge has three entrances, each on a different side of the swamp and each offering a different perspective on the place the Indians named the "Land of Trembling Earth."

On the north side is the Okefenokee Swamp Park. The 1,200-acre park offers the most family-friendly introduction to the swamp.

Water lilies and other water-loving flora flourish in the 412,000-acre South Georgia swamp called the Okefenokee National Wildlife Refuge.

It includes a ninety-foot observation tower, twenty-five-minute boat tour, reptile show, reconstructed pioneer homestead, animal exhibits, lectures, wildlife shows, and $7 canoe rentals.

Although situated outside the seven-hundred-square-mile swamp, the park does offer two-hour deep swamp excursions, depending on the water level and seating availability. The cost is $10 per person, and reservations are required by phone at least two days in advance. One-hour tours are also available on a first-come basis for $6 per person.

There are no overnight facilities at the Okefenokee Swamp Park, but the nearby Laura S. Walker Park has tent, camper, and primitive cabin sites available. The cabins are rustic: no lamps, no linens, no bathrooms.

The centerpiece of the 385-acre state park is its 111-acre lake that is used for skiing, fishing, and boating. Its swimming pool and game room are open during the summer only, but the 1.2-mile nature trail is accessible year-round.

Headwaters of the Suwanee River, the Okefenokee Swamp is the user-friendly refuge of alligators and other amphibians.

On the west side of the Okefenokee Swamp is the Stephen C. Foster State Park, which offers fully equipped cabins and campsites, but no swimming pool. The eighty-acre state park has a one-half-mile nature trail and twenty-five miles of day-use waterways. You can rent a canoe or motorboat, or take one of the three daily guided boat tours that last between sixty and ninety minutes.

One of the guides is corporate dropout Sue Lampert, who left the big-city life with an Atlanta insurance company to become a state park naturalist.

"When we come to a state park or nature refuge we are trying to get away from the concrete, computers, and technology and connect to the more natural rhythms in our bodies," Lampert said.

"We should be concerned about preserving our natural resources so we have places like this to go back to. The concrete and technology will not go away, but the natural resources are vanishing pretty quickly."

On the east side of the Okefenokee are the remnants of one man's early attempts to tame the swamp with technology. The Suwannee Canal Recreation Area centers around a twelve-mile-long canal left behind from an attempt in the 1880s to drain the swamp. Today, the canal provides a wet highway for boaters, fishers, and tourists.

The U.S. Fish and Wildlife Service, which runs the recreation area, offers overnight canoe trips and two- to five-day canoeing and camping trips (reservations required). Canoe rentals range from $10.75 for day trips to $61.25 for the five-day trips. Reservations must be made by telephone sixty days in advance through the range manager's office, which is open from 7 A.M. to 3:30 P.M., Monday through Friday.

Guided boat tours also are available at prices ranging from $7 a person for a one-hour tour to $14 a person for a night boat tour.

The Canal Recreation Concession rents just about everything you'll need for camping, canoeing, or boating: sleeping bags, tents, Coleman stoves and lanterns, ponchos, and portable toilets. They even rent bicycles ($1.50 per hour). But bring your own mosquito repellent; you can never have enough in a swamp.

SUWANNEE CANAL RECREATION AREA
Route 2, P.O. Box 336
Folkston, GA 31537
(912) 496-7156
Refuge Manager
P.O. Box 338
Folkston, GA 31537
(912) 496-3331

HOURS: Daily, 7 A.M. to 7:30 P.M., March 1 to Sept. 10; Daily, 8 A.M. to 6 P.M., Sept. 11 to Feb. 28.
ADMISSION: $3 per car.
HANDICAPPED ACCESS: Yes.
FOOD: Snack bar.
RESTROOMS: Yes.

STEPHEN C. FOSTER STATE PARK
Fargo, GA 31631
(912) 637-5274

HOURS: Daily, 7 A.M. to 7 P.M., Sept. 15 to March 1; Daily, 6:30 A.M. to 8:30 P.M., March 2 to Sept. 14.

ADMISSION: $3 per car entrance fee to National Wildlife Refuge, but no charge for the state park.

HANDICAPPED ACCESS: Handicapped camping spaces available.

FOOD: Small convenience store; no restaurants; nearest gas stations and grocery stores are twenty miles away.

RESTROOMS: Yes.

OKEFENOKEE SWAMP PARK
5700 Okefenokee Swamp Park
Waycross, GA 31501
(912) 283-0583

HOURS: Daily, 9 A.M. to 6:30 P.M., June to August; Daily, 9 A.M. to 5:30 P.M., September to May.

ADMISSION: Adults, $8; Children 5–11, $6; Seniors 62 and older, $7.

HANDICAPPED ACCESS: Yes.

FOOD: Snack bar.

RESTROOMS: Yes.

LAURA S. WALKER STATE PARK
Waycross, GA 31501
(912) 287-4900

HOURS: Daily, 7 A.M. to 10 P.M.

ADMISSION: $2 per car.

HANDICAPPED ACCESS: Yes.

FOOD: Snack bar.

RESTROOMS: Yes.

CHAPTER SIX

CHATTANOOGA

IT TOOK SHERMAN FOUR MONTHS TO TRAVEL between Chattanooga and Atlanta, but you can do it in two hours. You'll be rewarded with some of the finer attractions in the Southeast.

The new Tennessee Aquarium is superb—a means to understand, visually and intuitively, the life of the Tennessee River. The river itself merits exploration, too: cruise it, walk across it, or hike around an island that serves, in the middle of the city, as a sanctuary for wildlife.

The Houston Antique Museum left us breathless. It is a testament both to a gripping personal eccentricity and the beauty of the glassmaker's art.

Chattanooga is famous for its role in the Civil War. You can see the decisive battle of Chattanooga in miniature at Confederama, then ride the Incline Railway up Lookout Mountain and survey the battlefield for yourself.

And Chattanooga is the site of Rock City and Ruby Falls, examples of that which is most tacky, most touristy, and most fun about being on a family vacation.

Tennessee Aquarium

Chattanooga
113 miles

From Atlanta: Take Interstate 75 north. Just over the state line into Tennessee, take Interstate 24 west to U.S. Highway 27 north. Get off at Exit 1C. Follow the signs to the aquarium.

SURE, YOU'VE SEEN AQUARIUMS BEFORE— good ones, maybe even a great one. But unless you have been to Chattanooga, you have never see one like this.

The Tennessee Aquarium is the first major freshwater aquarium in the world. It traces the life and habitat of the Tennessee River, on whose banks it sits, from the headwaters in the mountains to the Gulf of Mexico.

There are no squid, no octopi. Instead, this is an aquarium with a story to tell, and the story has a plot. It begins in the hardwood forest of the Great Smoky Mountains, where the waters trickle and splash over smooth stones, and salamanders, snakes, songbirds, and river otters live.

The river grows deeper and wider; the story continues with largemouth bass and sixty-pound catfish. Farther on, in the delta, you see alligators, turtles, and water birds. The story concludes in the Gulf of Mexico with stingrays and sharks.

Another exhibit offers glimpses of life in other rivers of the world. You can see piranha, tigerfish, a boa constrictor.

A word to the wise: You will not be the only one to have heard that the aquarium is worth seeing. The place drew a million visitors the first six months it was open, and it continues to draw large crowds. Buy time-certain tickets over the phone in advance with a credit card. Otherwise, you will likely stand in line for quite a while to buy tickets for an entry scheduled a few hours after that.

A young visitor waves to a diver at the Tennessee Aquarium—the finest fresh-water aquarium in the world.

In any event, while waiting to tour the aquarium, you can while away some pleasant moments at Ross's Landing Park and Plaza (Ross's Landing was the original name of Chattanooga). The four-acre park features artificial streams in which children may wade. Minstrels play with guitar cases open for donations. Raised planted arches provide views of the river. Snack wagons and benches provide a place to eat lunch.

Also in the park is the city's new visitor center. The ground floor has stores and a food court. The second floor has more brochures on local attractions than you can carry out by yourself. You can touch TV screens to get specific kinds of information (shopping, accommodations, attractions); you can also approach polite live human beings who also answer your questions.

TENNESSEE AQUARIUM
One Broad Street
P.O. Box 11048
Chattanooga, TN 37401-2048
(615) 265-0695 or 1-800-262-0695

(You can buy advance time-certain tickets from these numbers using American Express, VISA, MasterCard, or Discover.)

HOURS: 10 A.M. to 6 P.M. From May 1 through Labor Day, the aquarium stays open until 8 P.M on Friday, Saturday, Sunday, and holidays. Closed Thanksgiving and Christmas.
ADMISSION: Adults, $8.75; Children 3–12, $4.75; Children 2 and younger, free.
HANDICAPPED ACCESS: Yes.
FOOD: At the visitor center.
RESTROOMS: Yes.

Houston Antique Museum/ Hunter Museum of Art/River Gallery

Chattanooga
113 miles

From the Tennessee Aquarium: Drive down Broad Street with the aquarium at your back. Turn left onto Fourth Street. Turn left onto High Street. At the end of High Street, you will see both museums and the gallery.

THESE THREE ATTRACTIONS FOR ART LOVERS sit cheek by jowl on a bluff above the Tennessee River not far from the aquarium. If you want an experience unlike any you are likely to have elsewhere, visit the Houston Antique Museum. For a high quality, if more generic, art museum located in a spectacular setting, the Hunter Museum is the place to go. If you love art and your credit card has a high limit, stop in at the River Gallery.

In truth, for art lovers, there is no need to pick. The three are so close to one another you will want to visit them all.

Houston Antique Museum

NOT EVEN LIFE ITSELF MATTERED MORE TO Anna Safley Houston than her collection of antiques. This eccentric woman collected millions of dollars worth of glassware while dying in poverty of malnutrition. To enter the Houston museum is to feel the obsession that gripped this eccentric woman.

The Houston Antique Museum houses the stunning glassware collection of "Antique Annie," who died rather than sell a single one of her thousands of pieces to pay for the medical care she needed.

The collection is stunning. "Antique Annie," as she was known, may have been half a bubble off plumb, but these are not garage sale knick-knacks. If you have not been here, you cannot imagine how many varieties of ornate glass pitchers have been created. Glass flowers wind around handles. The glass varies in color and texture and shape. Many of the pieces have great beauty and grace.

But the real story is not the glassware; it is Annie Houston. Little is known about her life; a historian is on the case. She was born in 1876. She married ten times, keeping the name Houston in honor of her favorite husband. In 1920, she opened an antique shop, but she lost it in the Depression. She lived in a barn after that, sleeping on the floor while her 15,000 glass pitchers hung from the ceiling. Near the end, she needed medical care, but she was unwilling to sell even a single item to raise the money. She died in 1951.

The collection this impoverished woman amassed is so extensive that only 10 percent of it can be displayed in the mansion that houses the museum. The other 90 percent is in the basement. Besides glassware, the museum displays ceramics, textiles, and some of Houston's beautiful old American furniture.

A tour begins with a videotape about Houston. In an upstairs room, pitchers hang from the ceiling, as they did in Houston's barn. Look at them, and an eerie feeling comes over you as you contemplate the life of this strange, obsessed, and gifted woman.

HOUSTON ANTIQUE MUSEUM
210 High Street
Chattanooga, TN 37403
(615) 267-7176

HOURS: Tuesday through Saturday, 10 A.M. to 4:30 P.M.;
    Sunday, 2 P.M. to 4:30 P.M. Closed Monday and holidays.
ADMISSION: $2 donation suggested.
HANDICAPPED ACCESS: No.
FOOD: No.
RESTROOMS: Yes.

Hunter Museum of Art

THIS MUSEUM SITS IN A MANSION ATOP A ninety-foot limestone cliff that rises straight above the Tennessee River. The view is breathtaking.

The interior view is fine, too. The mansion is linked to a more contemporary building, and the combined 50,000 square feet house an excellent collection.

The museum displays bronze statues by Frederic Remington of cowboys astride leaping horses, shooting wildly into the air. Old photographs by the Tennessee Valley Authority show the area and its people earlier this century. Photographs by Henri Cartier-Bresson, Edward Weston, Alfred Stieglitz, and Ansel Adams are hung. There are oils, by Thomas Hart Benton and many others, as well as sculpture, Japanese art, native American artifacts, and mobiles by Alexander Calder.

Group tours are free but must be arranged ten days in advance by calling the education assistant at (615) 267-0968.

HUNTER MUSEUM OF ART
10 Bluff View
Chattanooga, TN 37403
(615) 267-0968

HOURS: Tuesday through Saturday, 10 A.M. to 4:30 P.M.; Sundays, 1:30 P.M. to 4:30 P.M. Closed Monday and holidays.
ADMISSION: Free (requested donation of $2 for adults and $1 for children).
HANDICAPPED ACCESS: Yes.
FOOD: No.
RESTROOMS: Yes.

River Gallery

IF THE HUNTER AND HOUSTON HAVE WHETTED your appetite for art ownership, stop in at the River Gallery, a half-step away. Here you can buy jewelry, pottery, wood carvings, and expensive glasswork—into the $3,000 range. We gasped, too, but it's beautiful stuff.

RIVER GALLERY
River Gallery
400 East Second Street
Chattanooga, TN 37403
(615) 267-7353

HOURS: Monday through Saturday, 10 A.M. to 5 P.M.; Sunday, 1 P.M. to 5 P.M. Closed Easter, Thanksgiving, Christmas, and New Year's.

The Tennessee River

CHATTANOOGA IS KNOWN FOR THE CHOO-choo but dominated by the river. The *Southern Belle* and the *Chattanooga Star* offer riverboat cruises, some with food, some without. The historic Walnut Street Bridge, newly restored for pedestrian traffic only, provides views up and down the river for those with less time. The Maclellan Island wildlife sanctuary gives a glimpse of what life along the river used to be like before humans bottled it up in fancy aquariums and paved over the rest.

Southern Belle

Sails from the foot of Chestnut Street in downtown Chattanooga, on the riverbank just below the Tennessee Aquarium. Easy walking distance. From the aquarium: With the aquarium at your back, turn right onto Second Street. Turn left onto Riverfront Parkway; the parking lot will be immediately on your right.

THE 500-PASSENGER *SOUTHERN BELLE* OFFERS a bewildering array of cruises: lunch cruises, sightseeing cruises, Dixieland dinner cruises, moonlight cruises, Nashville Nite BBQ cruises, and more.

The sightseeing cruise is a pleasant way to spend an hour and a half. Sights to be seen include Hunter Museum, in a mansion high on a bluff above the river; Maclellan Island; and Lookout Mountain and Missionary Ridge, each the site of an important Civil War battle.

The interesting sights end before the cruise does, however, leaving the announcer with little to draw your attention besides the local gravel company. Still, boating down the river is relaxing.

Make your own choice, but there is one drawback to buying a ticket that includes a meal: You'll be downstairs in the dining room, looking out one window while, inevitably, the announcer describes a spectacular view on the other side of the boat. Also, for lunch at least, the food is nothing to write home about. Better, perhaps, to pay less and station yourself on the upper deck. (Another option is to hustle through the buffet line and carry your lunch up to one of the upper deck tables.)

Make reservations a week or more in advance; a credit card is necessary. You're supposed to arrive half an hour before the ship leaves the dock. It's not necessary, but if you are taking one of the meal cruises, the window seats go early.

CHATTANOOGA RIVERBOAT COMPANY
201 Riverfront Parkway
Pier 2
Chattanooga, TN 37402-1616
(615) 266-4488

HOURS: During the summer, the first sightseeing cruise leaves at 10 A.M. The final cruise of the day, the moonlight cruise, leaves at 10 P.M. Hours and available cruises vary according to season, so call ahead.
PRICES: $6.50 to $25.85, not including tax and tip, depending on which cruise you take.
HANDICAPPED ACCESS: Yes.
FOOD: Yes.
RESTROOMS: Yes.

Chattanooga Star

Sails from under the Walnut Street Bridge on the north shore of the river, the opposite side from the aquarium and the Southern Belle. *From the Tennessee Aquarium: With the aquarium at your back, turn left at Second Street. Turn left at Market Street. Cross the river on the Market Street*

Bridge. After crossing, turn immediately right onto Frazier Avenue. Go two tenths of a mile. Turn right onto Tremont Street, which leads straight to the boat.

THE *CHATTANOOGA STAR* IS SMALLER THAN the *Southern Belle*, funkier, less formal. It is powered by paddle-wheels on each side, in contrast to the *Southern Belle*, which is propelled from beneath the surface. The *Star* offers hour-long cruises, rather than 90 minutes, and you can order catered meals. A starlight cruise is available, with a live band and a cash bar.

One advantage of the *Star* is that during the day it stops at Maclelland Island, an eighteen-acre wildlife sanctuary in the middle of the river, smack in downtown Chattanooga. The *Star* is the only way you are permitted to get to the island; if you want to tour the sanctuary, skip the *Southern Belle* and take your tour aboard the *Chattanooga Star*.

CHATTANOOGA STAR
10 Tremont Street
P.O. Box 4522
Chattanooga, TN 37405
(615) 265-4522

HOURS: Wednesday through Saturday, departs hourly on the half-hour between 10:30 A.M. and 2:30 P.M. On Sunday, the *Star* departs hourly on the half-hour between 12:30 P.M. and 3:30 P.M.; the 3:30 departure will not drop you off at Maclellan Island. The last pick-up from the island is at 4 P.M. The starlight cruise departs Saturday at 10 P.M., with boarding at 9:30. Charters for meals are also available.
PRICES: One-hour boat ride, $5 for adults, $3 for children 4–12. (Price does not include $2 for the optional tour of Maclellan Island.) Meal cruises, available only on a charter basis, range from $13 per person for lunch to $27 for a prime rib dinner. Starlight cruise is $8.
HANDICAPPED ACCESS: No.
FOOD: On chartered cruises.
RESTROOMS: Yes.

Maclellan Island

The only way to get to the island is aboard the Chattanooga Star *(see previous page).*

WE HAVE ENJOYED FORESTS MANY TIMES AND many places, but something still thrills us about walking through a wildlife habitat in the middle of a major city.

So it is with Maclellan Island. Possums live here, along with raccoons, squirrels, muskrats, rabbits, beavers, and even a family of foxes. One end of the island cradles a rookery for great blue heron. Right in downtown Chattanooga.

Not that you'll see all these animals. This is no petting zoo. But even if you don't, enjoy the knowledge that they're there, peeping out at you from behind the leaves.

When you get off the *Chattanooga Star*, you'll be met by a naturalist from the Chattanooga Audubon Society (not affiliated, incidentally, with the National Audubon Society). The naturalist will give you materials to take on your self-guided tour of the island. Among these is a brochure with information keyed to signs along the paths. The brochure will help you spot signs of the animals, even if you never see the critters themselves.

MACLELLAN ISLAND
Chattanooga Audubon Society
900 North Sanctuary Road
Chattanooga, TN 37421
(615) 892-1499

HOURS: Must arrive aboard the *Chattanooga Star*; see departure times above. In June, July, and August, the island is open Wednesday through Sunday. In May and September, the island is open on weekends only. The rest of the year, it is used for school programs.

ADMISSION: $2, not including the price of the boat ride to the island.

HANDICAPPED ACCESS: No.

FOOD: No.

RESTROOMS: Yes.

Walnut Street Bridge

*From the Tennessee Aquarium: With the aquarium at your
back, turn left and walk up Second Street. Turn left onto
Walnut Street, which turns into the bridge.*

LET'S SUPPOSE YOU DO NOT GO IN FOR RIVER-
boat rides. You have no desire to walk the trails of a wooded island.
Yet you'd still like to get a look at the Tennessee River.

We recommend the Walnut Street Bridge.

The bridge opened in 1891 and was once a Chattanooga
thoroughfare. But it was scheduled to be torn down in 1978 after
officials deemed it unsafe. Instead, $4 million was raised to restore
the bridge for pedestrian use. It is 2,370 feet long; city officials call
it a "linear park" and say it is the longest pedestrian bridge in the
world. It is now covered with wood instead of asphalt, and has
benches on which to sit and gaze at the river.

It's good for jogging, too.

Chattanooga Choo-Choo
Holiday Inn/Shops

From the Tennessee Aquarium: With the aquarium at your back, drive east down Market Street. The Choo-Choo is on your left after 2.5 miles. A shuttle bus also makes the run regularly.

THE FIRST TRAIN TO OFFER PASSENGER SERVICE to the South departed Cincinnati, Ohio, on March 5, 1880. A newspaper reporter, in probably the most memorable phrase he ever turned, dubbed the little steam engine the Chattanooga Choo-Choo.

The phrase was immortalized by Glen Miller, who in 1941 composed "The Chattanooga Choo-Choo" for the film *Sun Valley Serenade.* The song sold a million copies; Miller was awarded the record industry's first gold record.

Today, the Chattanooga Choo-Choo refers to the Holiday Inn that has taken over the historic train depot and refurbished train cars as hotel rooms. Numerous shops operate here: a candy store, an ice cream parlor, some restaurants, and others.

If you don't mind your hotel room long and narrow, a night in one of the rail cars is a unique experience. They are quaintly furnished in an antique style, and they offer all the comforts of a regular hotel room. But you're definitely in a train car. Extra blankets and pillows are stored on the overhead racks, which once held the suitcases of railway travelers.

The lobby occupies the waiting room of the depot, which was built in the early 1900s. The eighty-five foot dome is supposed to be the "highest free-standing dome in the world," though we're not sure what that means.

In the courtyard, along with formal gardens and the train cars, you can find a statue of James Andrews, the man who led Union spies on a futile but exciting effort to steal a Confederate engine called the General. (See Big Shanty Museum, page 130.)

Also note that a $1 shuttle bus (fifty cents for kids six through twelve) will take you from the Choo-Choo to Confederama and the Incline Railway. (You can then ride the Incline Railway up Lookout Mountain and take a bus from the top to Ruby Falls and Rock City.)

CHATTANOOGA CHOO-CHOO
400 Market Street
Chattanooga, TN 37402
(615) 266-5000

PRICES: $105 per night for a railway-car room; $75–85 for more
   conventional rooms.
HANDICAPPED ACCESS: Yes.
FOOD: Yes.
RESTROOMS: Yes.

Confederama

From the Tennessee Aquarium: With the aquarium at your back, drive down Broad Street. About 4 miles later, get on Tennessee Avenue as it forks to the left (there are signs for Confederama and the Incline Railway). Confederama is a block and a half down on the left.

CONFEDERAMA, NEAR THE FOOT OF THE IN-cline Railway up Lookout Mountain, is the place to go if you want a better understanding of the Battle of Chattanooga. The battle was a turning point in the war (one of several, admittedly) that began with the Union troops under siege in Chattanooga, desperate, reduced to eating one-quarter of their normal rations each day. It ended with the Union forces breaking out of Chattanooga, which led to the fall of Atlanta, which led to Lincoln's re-election, which led to . . . well, by this time we have all heard what the outcome was.

The show begins with the theme from *Gone With the Wind*. Visitors sit around a three-dimensional, 480-square-foot reproduc-tion of the terrain—the Tennessee River, Lookout Mountain, Mis-sionary Ridge, and smaller hills from which Gen. U. S. Grant directed the battle. Five thousand miniature soldiers are on the battlefield. Blue lights flash to indicate the Union positions; red lights indicate the Confederate lines. Miniature cannon puff real smoke. A narrator explains it all.

Despite the potential of a diorama such as this, we found the narration a touch confusing. The narrator also betrays sympathy for the Confederates rather than neutrality, but what did you expect? You are in Dixie. Those minor points aside, Confederama is an interesting and informative show.

CONFEDERAMA
3742 Tennessee Avenue
Chattanooga, TN 37409
(615) 821-2812

HOURS: Summer, from the end of school through Labor Day: Monday through Saturday, 8:30 A.M. to 8:30 P.M.; Sunday, 9:30 A.M. to 8:30 P.M. The rest of the year: Monday through Saturday, 9 A.M. to 5 P.M.; Sunday, 12:30 P.M. to 5 P.M.

ADMISSION: Adults, $4; Children 3–12, $2.

HANDICAPPED ACCESS: Yes.

FOOD: Soft drinks, candy, chips.

RESTROOMS: Yes.

Lookout Mountain Incline Railway

Follow the directions to Confederama. Two-tenths of a mile farther, on the right, you will see the base of the railway.

BILLED AS THE STEEPEST PASSENGER RAILWAY in the world and America's most amazing mile, the Incline Railway runs up the side of Lookout Mountain and offers a spectacular view of the valley below.

It is steep enough that the cars are not built flat, but on an 18-degree angle: when the ground is flat, the cars tilt.

We'll grant that it's steep, but, for the faint of heart, we deem it not to be scary. Unlike the cog railway up Mount Washington in New Hampshire, this never rises above timber line. You never feel as if you are clinging to the face of a cliff.

The incline is hauled up the mountain by cables, like an elevator. There are two cars, one on each end of the cable; they pass each other exactly halfway up the mountain.

From the top, on a clear day you can see—not forever, but five states: both Carolinas, Tennessee, Georgia, and Alabama. Three blocks from the top, you can visit Point Park, run by the National Park Service, and see the location where the "Battle Above the Clouds" was fought in 1863. (If you went to Confederama before you got on the Incline, you know about that.)

From Memorial Day through Labor Day, a shuttle bus runs from the top of the railway to both Ruby Falls and Rock City. It costs twenty-five cents a trip. You can take the train to the top, see the sights, and use the other half of your round trip to get back down.

LOOKOUT MOUNTAIN INCLINE RAILWAY
827 East Brow Road
Lookout Mountain, TN 37350
(615) 821-4224

HOURS: Between Labor Day and Memorial Day, 8:30 A.M. to
9:20 P.M. The winter hours are 9 A.M. to 5:20 P.M.
PRICES: Adults, $6 round trip, $5 one way; Children 3–12, $3
round trip, $2.50 one way; Children 2 and younger, free.
HANDICAPPED: Yes.
FOOD: Sub shop at the bottom, ice cream parlor at top.
RESTROOMS: Yes.

Passengers on the Lookout Mountain Incline Railway enjoy the spectacular view as they approach the top of what is called America's most amazing mile.

Ruby Falls

From the Tennessee Aquarium: With the aquarium behind you, head out Broad Street and follow the signs to Ruby Falls. It is about six miles away. Ruby Falls can also be reached by riding the Incline Railway up Lookout Mountain and taking a shuttle bus.

THE THING ABOUT RUBY FALLS IS THAT THERE is nothing ruby about them. They're not red at all; they're as clear as water usually is, so don't be disappointed. They were named for the wife of the man who discovered them.

Freed from that misconception, you're ready now to enjoy the tour. Yes, Ruby Falls is touristy. Yes, everybody who visits Chattanooga on vacation goes there. Yes, you might encounter long lines of people wearing cameras and Bermuda shorts. Go anyway. Take the kids. It's fun.

The falls were discovered in 1928. A large cave in the side of Lookout Mountain had once been used as a Confederate hospital, but train tracks had closed the entrance. A group of entrepreneurs decided to sink an elevator shaft 420 feet down into the mountain to the cave.

But at 260 feet, they hit a small opening. One of the entrepreneurs, Leo Lambert, crawled through. When he returned seventeen hours later, he told of having found a spectacular underground waterfall. No one believed him, so he took his wife, Ruby, on his second trip to verify his story.

Your tour guide will lead you through the cave's passages—it's about a one-mile round trip—pointing out rock formations that resemble bacon, potato chips, an angel's wing, whatever. Before you enter the cavern where the water falls, the lights go black. The theme from *2001: A Space Odyssey* fills the room, to give you the proper sense of awe. Then the lights blaze on and there it is, a 145-foot waterfall with no known source, 1,120 feet under the mountain (which has risen higher above you as you walked toward its center). On their last day on the job, tour guides sometimes jump into the pool at the base of the falls in a farewell ritual.

Atop the cave is a lookout tower and a children's playground with balls, tunnels, and slides.

RUBY FALLS
Route 4, Scenic Highway
Chattanooga, TN 37409
(615) 821-2544

HOURS: Memorial Day through Labor Day, 8 A.M. to 9 P.M. November through March, 8 A.M. to 6 P.M. In September, October, April, and May, 8 A.M. to 8 P.M. Open every day except Christmas.

ADMISSION: Adults, $7.75; Seniors 62 and older, $6.75; Children 6–12, $3.50.

HANDICAPPED ACCESS: No.

FOOD: Coffee shop and deli.

RESTROOMS: Yes.

Rock City

*From the Tennessee Aquarium: With the aquarium at your
back, drive down Broad Street 3 miles. Turn left at the
overhead sign to Rock City. Take a right at the next traffic
light. Follow that road up the mountain. Take a left at the top
of the mountain; drive 6 miles to Rock City.*

SURELY, THIS IS ONE OF THE MORE UNUSUAL
tourist attractions in the area. It is a bizarre amalgamation of huge
boulders, flowers, a swaying bridge, breathtaking vistas, strange-
looking deer, and children's fairy tales.

Rock City, just over the Georgia state line from Tennessee,
began as Frieda Carter's garden. Her husband, Garnet Carter,
improved the pine-needle path among the boulders and opened the
garden to the public in 1932. An unusual advertising campaign
secured Rock City's place as a bit of Americana: "See Rock City"
was painted on the roofs of more than 900 barns in states ranging
from Michigan to Florida. (The campaign ended in 1965, a victim
of Lady Bird Johnson's Beautification Act.)

You start your tour on a path, now made of slate, that winds
among gigantic boulders green and furry with moss. At a couple of
points the space between the stones is extremely narrow; this is not
recommended for the claustrophobic or the obese. At one point,
you pass an enclosure of white fallow deer, which look to the
untutored eye like goats.

The path forks; you must choose between a stone bridge and a
long suspension bridge. The suspension bridge is fun, but be
warned: Pranksters ahead of you may try to bounce the bridge as
much as they can. If heights make you queasy, choose the solidity of
stone.

Soon you emerge onto a boulder projecting from the mountainside from which, on a clear day, you can see seven states:

From this rock outcropping at Rock City, which is called Lover's Leap, visitors on a clear day can see seven states.

Tennessee, Kentucky, Virginia, North Carolina, South Carolina, Georgia, and Alabama. Or so they say; it all looked kind of like distance to us.

The tour concludes through a manmade cave called Fairyland Caverns, which features three-dimensional tableaux of numerous fairy tales, such as a wax Hansel and Gretel about to enter the gingerbread house. Children love it.

ROCK CITY
Dept. B
Lookout Mountain, GA 30750
(706) 820-2531

HOURS: 8:30 A.M. until sundown; open every day except Christmas.

ADMISSION: Adults, $7.95; Children 3–12, $3.95; Children 2 and younger, free.

HANDICAPPED ACCESS: An abbreviated tour to the spectacular view is available for those in wheelchairs, free of charge.

FOOD: Yes.

RESTROOMS: Yes.

Lookout Mountain Flight Park

From Chattanooga: Take Interstate 24 west. Go 17.1 miles. Get off at Exit 167 and take Interstate 59 south. Go 7.8 miles, then get off at Exit 2. Turn left at the end of the exit ramp. Go three-tenths of a mile, then turn right at the stop light onto Highway 11. Go one-tenth of a mile, then turn left at the blinking light onto 136. Go 1.1 miles, then turn left onto Piney Road. Go 4.7 miles, then, at the top of the mountain, turn right at the stop sign onto 189. Go six-tenths of a mile. The flight park is on your right.

From Rock City, the flight park can be reached by turning left out of Rock City and following the signs that say "Hang Gliding."

EVEN IF YOU HAVE NEVER BEEN HANG GLIDING, you can soar hundreds of feet above the earth. You do it by taking a tandem flight, in which you and your instructor hang from the same glider. The instructor's job is to fly the thing and get it down safely. Your job is to hang there and enjoy the view. We've tried it (elsewhere, not here), and it's exhilarating. The ride feels stable, not fluttery, and the landings are feather-light.

You become airborne either by walking off the edge of the mountain, 1,340 feet above the valley below, or by being towed by an ultralight aircraft. Before and after the flight, you can watch experienced gliders riding updrafts to soar hundreds of feet above the mountain. Other gliders will fly off into the distance; people have launched from this spot and flown to points south of Atlanta, which is more than ninety miles distant.

Pilots rated at least at a novice level (or higher, depending on weather conditions) by the U.S. Hang Gliding Association can rent equipment and fly on their own.

A hang glider takes off at Lookout Mountain Flight Park, preparing to ride the updrafts at one of the nation's premier hang gliding locations.

The center also offers lessons on a bunny hill in gliders equipped with training wheels.

Make reservations. The center is particularly busy on weekends. We were brusquely treated, despite having arranged our visit in advance. We trust you will fare better. It is a lovely spot, one of the premier hang gliding locations in the country.

LOOKOUT MOUNTAIN FLIGHT PARK
Route 2, P.O. Box 215-H
Rising Fawn, GA 30738
(706) 398-3541

HOURS: Pro shop and office open 9 A.M. to 6 P.M. every day
except Wednesday. Call to make reservations for a specific
time; $25 deposit via credit card required.

PRICE: Tandem flight (10 minutes or so), $99. Half-day lesson,
including five bunny-hill flights, $99. Other packages cover
two days, several tandem flights, etc., and range up to $799
for the deluxe beginner-to-solo package.

HANDICAPPED ACCESS: No.

FOOD: No.

RESTROOMS: Outhouse.

CONCLUSION

GEORGIA REWARDS RICHLY THOSE WHO EX-
plore it. Visit the places listed in this book and you will discover,
as we have, a state that exists simultaneously in the past and the
present.

You will find a state steeped in history, shaped by both triumph
and defeat. Within a day's drive of Atlanta, you can travel back in
time to the site of America's earliest gold rush, or stroll among the
graves and fortifications of the war that tore the nation apart.

You can visit the birthplace of a civil rights leader or that of
the Cherokee nation. These, for many, are places of pilgrimage;
people visit them not only to amuse and educate themselves, but
also to feel a personal connection to history.

You can witness, too, today's history unfold from the studios of
CNN, and walk the same halls as the current governor of Georgia.
You can tour the city that will host the Centennial Olympic
games—in itself a magnificent blend of past and future wrapped
into a single event.

This book is built around Atlanta, just as the state itself seems
to radiate from the Capital of the South. Highways encircle the city
and then extend to all corners of the state, making nearly every site
and attraction accessible within a day's drive.

Atlanta is not only the economic epicenter of Georgia, but its
symbolic essence as well. It is a place both old and new at the same
time.

If you have visited Underground Atlanta, you know what we
mean. Taking the abandoned core of the original city—the end-of-
the-road railroad town called Terminus—Atlanta has created an
artificial heart for its modern downtown. Underground Atlanta is
both a mall for tourists and a civic focal point and gathering spot for
a metropolitan area that continues to spiral outward.

Perhaps you have discovered by now that Georgia is a place of
many great men and women, and a few eccentrics. This is a state

that inspires visionaries. Some chose the bullet, others the ballot, some the paintbrush, and some the defiance of civil disobedience. All have left behind something for the rest of us to consider.

If you have visited the birthplace of President Jimmy Carter, you have seen just how long a journey it is from rural Georgia to the world stage. If you have visited Franklin Roosevelt's Little White House, you have sensed how Georgia could help a president escape the cares of office when the world was at war.

And if you have visited Howard Finster's art studio, you have felt what it means to be held in the grip of splendid inspiration, covering everything in your path with art that seems to spew forth in a torrent.

Some of those who shaped Georgia also had the foresight to leave it alone. Theme parks are thrilling, and water parks exciting, and Georgia has both. But so are the mountains, rivers, swamps, and valleys that nature has created and mankind can never improve.

Part of the thrill of rafting on the Chattooga River, for example, is the rapids, as stomach-churning and heart-stopping as any amusement park ride. But the deeper thrill comes from rafting through woods on a beautiful river unspoiled by modern man.

Perhaps by now you have visited Chattanooga. If so, you have seen how Chattanooga and Atlanta are linked: by proximity, by history, by highway, and by a rail line that played a pivotal role in this nation's history. you may have seen on the miniature battlefield of Confederama how the federal troops broke out of Chattanooga and began the march that led to the fall of Atlanta, and ultimately to the fall of the Confederacy.

All along this rail line the battle raged. Again and again, the Union troops, in wide flanking maneuvers, threatened to cut the rail line to Atlanta that was the lifeline for the Confederate army. Again and again the rebels fell back to defend the rail line until at last their backs were pressed to the city of Atlanta itself.

Today the highway along this route carries thousands of visitors to the Tennessee Aquarium, one of the most modern and interesting in the world.

And if, in between, you stopped in Dalton, chances are you at least thought about buying some carpet, where an enormous modern industry has sprung from an old-time, living-room craft.

Georgia has always been a state of contrasts, contradictions, and conflicts. It is made of blood and ash and soil and water. It has been torn apart by guns and hatred; it has been rebuilt with compassion and reconciliation. No southern state, perhaps, was more ravaged by the Civil War; no other more healed by the balm of the Civil Rights movement.

It is a beautiful state with some ugly scars, but it does not hide or apologize for its past. Instead it lays itself out for anyone to see who cares to take the time to look.

INDEX

Jeff Kunerth is the demographics reporter for *The Orlando Sentinel*. Since joining the *Sentinel* in 1974, Kunerth has worked as an education reporter, feature writer, and columnist, and he headed the newspaper's Atlanta bureau for five years. He lives with his wife, Gretchen, and sons, Chad and Jesse, in Altamonte Springs, Florida.

Don Melvin is a general assignment reporter for *The Atlanta Journal-Constitution*. Prior to joining the *Journal-Constitution*, Melvin headed the Atlanta bureau for the Fort-Lauderdale *Sun-Sentinel* for four years. He has traveled widely throughout the United States and overseas. He lives in Marietta, Georgia, with his wife, Barbara Wolfe, and daughters, Jaime and Jennifer.